MW00390703

To the Temple
of Tranquility...
and Step On It!

Also by Ed Begley Jr.

Living Like Ed: A Guide to the Eco-Friendly Life

Ed Begley, Jr.'s Guide to Sustainable Living: Learning to Conserve Resources and Manage an Eco-Conscious Life

Ed Begley Jr.

A MEMOIR

To the Temple of Tranquility... and Step On It!

New York

Copyright © 2023 by Ed Begley Jr.

All photos courtesy of the author except where noted.

Jacket design by Amanda Kain

Jacket photograph © Everett Collection; back-of-jacket photograph © Tricia Lee Pascoe

Jacket copyright © 2023 by Hachette Book Group, Inc.

Hachette Book Group supports the right to free expression and the value of copyright. The purpose of copyright is to encourage writers and artists to produce the creative works that enrich our culture.

The scanning, uploading, and distribution of this book without permission is a theft of the author's intellectual property. If you would like permission to use material from the book (other than for review purposes), please contact permissions@hbgusa.com. Thank you for your support of the author's rights.

Hachette Books
Hachette Book Group
1290 Avenue of the Americas
New York, NY 10104
HachetteBooks.com
Twitter.com/HachetteBooks
Instagram.com/HachetteBooks

First Edition: October 2023

Published by Hachette Books, an imprint of Perseus Books, LLC, a subsidiary of Hachette Book Group, Inc. The Hachette Books name and logo is a trademark of the Hachette Book Group.

The Hachette Speakers Bureau provides a wide range of authors for speaking events. To find out more, go to hachettespeakersbureau.com or email HachetteSpeakers@hbgusa.com.

Books by Hachette Books may be purchased in bulk for business, educational, or promotional use. For information, please contact your local bookseller or Hachette Book Group Special Markets Department at: special.markets@hbgusa.com.

The publisher is not responsible for websites (or their content) that are not owned by the publisher.

Print book interior design by Amy Quinn

Library of Congress Control Number: 2023938640

ISBNs: 9780306832109 (hardcover), 9780306832123 (ebook), 9780306834080 (B&N.com signed edition)

Printed in the United States of America

LSC-C

Printing 1, 2023

To Allene, Jeanette, and Bruno, who have guided me every step of the way.

Contents

Permit Me

SITTING ALONE IN THE BACK of my father's hot car was nothing new for me.

Leaving your kids or pets inside a sweltering vehicle was not frowned upon in the midsixties. It was regarded as more of an impromptu spa day.

And, thrifty man that my dad was, he was not about to leave the motor running, even on a hot day in August.

Okay, I had a tendency to embellish back then. It was not August, but March. March 16, to be exact. My half birthday. Not quite sweet sixteen, but more than a quinceañera.

Though those two events are significant ones, I am aware that a fifteen-and-a-half-year birthday is not. And to celebrate such a non-event leaves you open to much derision.

As did complaining about a hot car when it's technically still winter in L.A.

(As did complaining about a hot planet a few years hence, but let me return to 1965.)

If you live in the Golden State and you reach fifteen and a half years of age, you are allowed to apply for a learner's permit with the Department of Motor Vehicles. Then, if you haven't killed anyone in those next six months, and you yourself live to see sixteen, you're given a full and proper license to operate a vehicle on the streets and freeways of Los Angeles.

Or in my case, Van Nuys. It's important to note that—despite my father's profession and his success—we did not live in Beverly Hills, where my father's car was now parked. We lived in the Valley, in a surprisingly modest home. Two bedrooms, 1,700 square feet.

But my father occasionally had his indulgences, and a Beverly Hills business manager was one of them.

And here my father came, document in hand. Walking away from the accountant's office as one would exit a structure engulfed in flames, though it most certainly was not . . . that was just the way my father walked. To the mailbox. To catch a subway in Manhattan. Getting to the podium to receive his Academy Award.

This allegro philosophy was not confined to his gait. It applied to meals: "I paid the check. Finish up and meet me in the car."

And vacations as well: "That's the Grand Canyon. Grab a shot and we'll try to make the Painted Desert by nightfall."

But on this particular day, I was quite grateful for his alacrity.

Because, as he jumped into the car and pulled away from the curb, he handed me the document that I needed to change my life, the document essential to all matters DMV in 1965, as it is today: my birth certificate.

As we wound our way back to the Valley over Coldwater Canyon, I began to really think through the nuts and bolts of the plan that my best friend, Dave Goodman, and I had hatched. Code name: Permit Me.

A full driver's license at age sixteen was certainly something to aspire to. You could take your friends to the beach or Disneyland. You could take a girl out on a date . . . without your parents or your bus pass. And the learner's permit was not the same, as it had this one serious restriction: You had to have a fully licensed adult in the car with you during those endless six months.

It also had this one wonderful and largely unknown loophole. You could use your learner's permit alone and unsupervised . . . if you're learning to drive a motorcycle.

And Dave and I loved our motorcycles. To be clear, we did not own motorcycles. We intended to rent them. By the hour. There was a rental outfit at Sepulveda and Oxnard that would rent you a 90cc Japanese motorcycle, if you could produce a scrap of paper known as a learner's permit. A document generated on an actual typewriter, and absent a photo of said applicant, or a California grizzly, or a prospector panning for gold, or anyone or anything that would keep us from creating the document on our own.

Go figure. I don't know why they thought Valley teens would return the bikes in the absence of photo ID and a credit card, and I don't know why we would have, but we always did.

For guys my age, these noisy contraptions somehow held the promise of speed, freedom . . . perhaps even romance! We had seen Steve McQueen jump that fence on his Triumph in *The Great Escape*. Marlon Brando rode his Triumph into town and into our collective psyche in *The Wild One*.

But those were golden screen moments from the past, and Dave and I tried to remain au courant, so we were both regular customers at the Fox Theater on Van Nuys Boulevard. Hardly art-house cinema, but they often ran films from avant-garde filmmakers, like Roger Corman.

We went multiple times to see *Hells Angels on Wheels*. Not so much for the movie but for this young actor who was in it. An actor who, like Marlon, had something unique and dangerous and wonderful going on. And, like Marlon, he would go on to win multiple Academy Awards and be regarded as one of the finest actors of my lifetime.

But for now, I was headed back to the Valley where I belonged. And it was then that I focused on the envelope that my dad had given me. The envelope that contained my birth certificate.

What did an ancient document from 1949 look like? Was it written on parchment with a quill? Did it have one of those cute little baby footprints that make being switched at birth less likely?

Before I could settle those very worthy questions, a quick inspection of said document caused a new question to move to the top of my queue, and it was a doozie.

"Dad?"

"Mm-hm."

"Why is there no mother's name on my birth certificate?"

My dad was not much for touchy-feely exchanges. But at least he didn't respond by going on the offensive with some version of "None of your fucking business!," which had been his default setting for such inquiries in the past.

In the minus column, he didn't feel the need to immediately respond, or to pull over. He just kept driving, occasionally looking in the mirror, and my immediate thought was:

How could he think this wouldn't come up, once I looked at the document?

Had he simply forgotten that my mother's name was not on it?

I knew who my mother was. Amanda Begley (née Huff). My father and Amanda had three children before she died of cancer in 1957. My brother Tom, my sister Allene, and me, the youngest.

After what seemed like an eternity, my father finally spoke.

"Amanda wasn't your mother."

As shocking as that was, I attempted to pick up the pace, making it less like NASA communicating with *Voyager I* as it heads into deep space, and more like an actual conversation.

"Who *is* my mother?"

Long pause. Finally:

"Sandy's your mother."

Now it was my turn to slow down. There would be no fiber-optic speeds coming from my side of the conversation now either. Just dial-up. 150 baud.

In that moment, it all made sense. I loved Sandy. A little eccentric, but fun. When I was much younger, we lived in Merrick, out on Long Island, so I often saw her at Christmas or Easter in the city. There was something about her. My sister once hopped the Long Island Rail Road, got to Grand Central Station, and started asking commuters where Sandy was. We saw her so much at that particular hub, we both thought she lived there.

If it ever occurred to my sister or me to ask, "Now, who is Sandy again?" . . . we never did. You were taught not to ask too many questions back then. Years later, I would learn that Sandy was a page at NBC that my father had taken up with, though he was quite actively married to another woman, Amanda.

To this day, I have no idea how much Amanda knew about Sandy or vice versa. But for now, me and my dad are stuck in the car together with this little bombshell.

We rode in silence the rest of the way to the DMV.

Had I achieved even a small dose of acceptance or gratitude at that point in my life, I would have seen this moment for what it was: a tremendous gift. Ten minutes ago, I had a mother who was dead. Now I had the live variety. All in all, a good day.

But acceptance and gratitude were seen as character defects among my peers, so I was not remotely ready for anything like that.

I would soon learn that nearly everyone but my sister and I knew this deep dark secret. And we both felt a deep betrayal as a result of it.

I was dumbfounded at my father's ability to pull off such a massive bit of deception, probably because I was so bad at that kind of thing.

I remember being asked by my fifth-grade teacher in Merrick if I had turned in my homework assignment, and you did not want to supply Sister Killean with the wrong answer. Roughly once a week, some unlucky youngster in her class would be bleeding from the knuckles, lip, or nose.

"I put it on your desk," I offered, sure that she would look more carefully and spot it among the many tests before her.

She scarcely glanced at the neat piles, arranged by row, and further alphabetized. "I can spot your chicken scratch from across the room. It's not here."

I was deeply confused by that. I had a very clear memory of placing it on her desk. Perhaps . . . ? I spotted the trash can beside her and offered an explanation:

"Oh . . . I'll bet it fell in the trash can. The wind . . . " I said, pointing to the nearby window.

She didn't afford me the courtesy of a glance at the nearby window, which was only slightly ajar. Perhaps because it was dead calm that morning.

I was trying her patience. She was beginning to finger her sturdy ruler, the way a mob enforcer would heft a small cudgel. "The only wind I hear is coming from your mouth. Where's the homework?"

There was a second trash can, near the door, and I think I even smacked my head to illustrate my foolishness. "I just cleaned out my desk . . . and my lunch box. I bet I accidentally threw it in there with my trash."

She looked at me, then at the trash can near the door, and sauntered over to it. After surveying the contents briefly from a standing position, she bent down and picked up the metal can while summoning me to join her with a crooked finger.

I walked over to her, puzzled as to what would come next. The can was indeed filled with desk and lunch box detritus, some of it malodorous in that close proximity.

She gently took my hand and led me out into the hall as the rest of the class looked on. Was this crazy woman going to sift through this fetid mess in search of a single page of long division to prove her point?

I got my answer quickly. With eyes fixed on me, she emptied its contents at my feet. "Find it. Bring it to me. Then clean up this mess."

As she headed back to her desk, she didn't even bother to close the door.

I started to weep at the injustice of it all, hoping Ilene McGlachlin didn't see me. I was planning on asking her out one day.

I distinctly remember the smell of the rotten lunch, some of it probably mine . . . as I looked at one, then another soggy piece of paper, desperate to find the missing assignment. I probably spent a full five minutes looking, when I stopped suddenly and realized . . . I was never going to find it.

For it was not in that particular trash can. Or the one that preceded it. It was not anywhere on the school grounds. I had not done said homework.

It was just another lie I concocted for Sister Killean. Like the many I told Jeanette, the woman who raised me after my mom (eventually demoted to stepmom) passed away. "Where did you get those quarters?" Jeanette asked me one day, as she eyed a stack of them on my dresser.

This was not an illogical question. As it was a time before I had a paper route, sold greeting cards door-to-door, or worked at Orange Julius or See's Candies. It was probably a decade before I first worked as an actor. A movie cost a quarter back then. You could get a steak with the buck-fifty that Jeanette now held.

"Robbie Blumenthal gave them to me," I offered casually, as I continued studying my Boy Scout manual. Guess I missed the chapter on honesty. But I was certain that this would end the line of questioning. Robbie and his brother Arthur were two of my best friends at the time. Their dad wasn't some fly-by-night actor. He had a steady job at Gimbels in Manhattan. I didn't find it illogical that they share some of their incredible wealth with me.

What Jeanette did next truly shocked me. She scooped up all six of the quarters, grabbed me by my ear, and led me over to Robbie's house a few doors down and knocked. Robbie appeared quickly, followed by his mother.

Before I could figure out just the right balance of banjo eyes and throat clearing that would get Robbie to go along, Jeanette took charge. "Did you give Eddie these quarters?" she said, holding them out for all to see.

And before Robbie had time to assess what answer would best serve me, his mother gave him a whack and seemed pained in asking, "You gave Eddie six quarters?" A simple "Ow! No!" was all he could offer under the circumstances.

And who could blame him, since of course, those quarters didn't come from Robbie. To my great shock and surprise, it was the same exact amount of money missing from a cup on my father's dresser.

So I was bad at lying. But that wasn't going to stop me from doing it. Hmm. If only I had some tool, some matter in a solid, liquid, or gaseous state that could give me the courage and the heightened awareness to be better at lying or in other stressful situations.

It didn't take me long to find it. It was, at first, stolen pills. Then stolen liquor. It was even occasionally the nitrous oxide pilfered from a can of Reddi-wip in the dairy aisle.

That covers it, right? The three states of matter. Solid. Liquid. Gas. Maybe I was going to pass that chemistry exam after all? So I developed a warped sense of reality for the next two decades. A warp fomented by a nearly daily regimen of drugs and alcohol from 1967 to 1979.

Now, I'd like to think I've become a better liar in the time that has transpired since the end of the tumultuous seventies, but you be the judge.

I'm going to list a bunch of true facts that I could have never imagined in 1965. But I swear to you on my life, they are 100 percent verifiably true.

Okay, one of them is a lie. See if you can spot it:

I would have a career that would span seven decades and include hundreds of movies and TV shows.

I would discover that my brother, Tom Begley, was my cousin, not my brother.

I would get to meet all four Beatles, and even get to be friends with them.

I would smoke a joint with Charles Manson at the Spahn Ranch in Chatsworth.

I would be stabbed, beaten, and hospitalized waiting for a bus in Los Angeles.

I would buy my first electric car in 1970.

I would have a much-improved electric car in 1993, one I sometimes charged at O. J. Simpson's house.

I would carry my dear friend Cesar Chavez through the streets of Delano.

I would serve several terms as governor in California, for a total of fifteen years.

I would regularly spend time with Groucho Marx in his home and occasionally enjoy a sleepover.

I would play Trivial Pursuit with the Clintons, and show them their first electric car.

I would get to know and work with Kirk Douglas, Meryl Streep, Peter Falk, Alan Arkin, Michael Caine, Billy Wilder, Richard Pryor, Dave Mamet, Jeff Goldblum, Eric Idle, Denzel Washington, Buck Henry, Don Henley, Jane Fonda, Geena Davis, Dabney Coleman, Lily Tomlin, Leonardo DiCaprio, Vince Gilligan, John Cleese, Danny Glover, Harvey Keitel, William Hurt, Larry Kasdan, Larry David, Anjelica Huston, Pam Grier, Penny Marshall, Alfre Woodard, Taylor Swift, Jeff Bridges, Yaphet Kotto, Rob Reiner, and Christopher Guest.

And most incredibly, at the very moment . . . the very second that my dad told me the shocking news about my mother, we passed a driveway that led to two separate houses in the vicinity of Coldwater and Mulholland.

A driveway that for over forty years was shared by Marlon Brando and that Roger Corman star on the motorcycle, Jack Nicholson. There would be many trips up and down that driveway over the years. You see, I worked at Art's Deli on Ventura and would deliver sandwiches to those talented gentlemen, and let me tell you, they were big tippers!

Okay, you probably figured out which one was bullshit:

Not the governor one. I said I served as governor *in* California, not *of* California. You'll soon learn governor of what.

It was that last one about Art's Deli. That was total bullshit.

I never brought Marlon or Jack sandwiches, though I probably should have. That's the kind of thing you do for friends.

I should probably also offer a word of explanation of the title of this book.

But not just yet.

I'm in no hurry.

Watts Line

THIS IS IT.

I could stop there and be done with this chapter, or this entire book for that matter, as that is probably the truest thing that I have ever said, or heard.

It is also the title of one of Alan Watts's many fine works, and I would urge every reader to stop reading my humble effort right now (you already paid for it, right?) and pick up a copy of any of the many books written by the great Alan Watts.

But before you exit the bookstore and hop on your bike to head home and read it (I can dream, can't I?), I'd ask that you really open your mind to what those words might mean.

This is it.

This moment, right now . . . is really all we have.

Though planning for the future and learning from the past have value, many of us spend far too much time focused on what has been, and what is to be, and in so doing, we fail to fully engage and commit to this moment, here it comes again . . . this one . . . right now.

. . . where we can make a conscious effort to embrace bliss. That "the spiritual is not to be separated from the material, nor the wonderful from the ordinary," as Alan Watts so ably put it.

But in my attempt to put his teachings into practice, I quickly realized that I could experience serenity more easily up at Big Sur, or in a yurt in Topanga. But I wasn't so good at it standing in line at the DMV. Or waiting for the agent's call after testing for a series.

I also then realized that the unthinkable had occurred . . . I had become my father's son. I ate fast, drove fast, moved fast, and lived fast. Yes, I wanted serenity, but I wanted it quickly.

To the Temple of Tranquility, and step on it!

And rather than put in the actual time to learn and implement the teachings of Alan Watts, Sai Baba, the Maharishi, or any of the spiritual masters I had become aware of at the time, I found it was much quicker and easier to find enlightenment under the gentle guidance of Messrs. Walker and Beam.

Johnnie Walker and Jim Beam, to be precise.

Why spend all that time (and fuel) to drive up to Tassajara and sit Zazen. A comfortable barstool could get you there so much quicker, and oh, the enlightened souls you'd meet along the way . . . like Alan Watts!

You'd have as good a chance of spotting him at a local pub as you would an ashram. The man liked his gargle. And so did I.

I wanted serenity in a bottle. And the truth is, it worked. I was such a wreck in my teens that alcohol probably saved me before it nearly killed me.

So this chapter on enlightenment and Alan Watts includes a lengthy quest to find tranquility in a tumbler. A quest that lasted from 1971 to 1979.

The student was ready, but would the master appear?

Appear he did. I soon became an eager disciple of Alan Watts's teachings as interpreted by one Harry Dean Stanton, who, like me, was on a nightly quest for the right combination of serenity and Stoli.

I first met Harry Dean at the Troubadour bar in 1972, and we became instant friends. Harry was a fine singer and an able guitarist, so we both were drawn to the Troubadour for its target-rich environment of available ladies, as well as the great music a few yards away in the showroom.

For a $4 cover, two-drink minimum, you could sit within a few feet of Elton John, Joni Mitchell, James Taylor, the Eagles, and hundreds of other huge stars from the sixties, the seventies, and beyond. And if you knew Bob Marchese or Kenny Saint John at the door, you could get one of those prime seats close to the stage.

But I sat in every part of that club, and there was no such thing as a bad seat.

And I wasn't always *in* the audience. I did stand-up comedy for several years in the sixties and seventies. I opened at the Troubadour for acts like Don McLean, Dave Mason, Canned Heat, and Neil Sedaka.

I performed for eighteen thousand people at the Nassau Coliseum as the opening act for Loggins and Messina, John Sebastian, and Poco.

I played at Max's Kansas City and the Bottom Line in New York. I played clubs and colleges and concerts all across the country, and was even part of a comedy duo for some time with Michael Richards. We appeared at the Troubadour together in 1969, and Doug Weston, the owner of the club, wanted to manage us.

And if the Troubadour wasn't enough to lure you to Santa Monica and Doheny, just two doors to the east sat Dan Tana's Italian Restaurant, where the kitchen was open till one a.m., and the bar till two (even later, if they got to know you). It was also a place where you could rub elbows with those same Troubadour artists after they finished their set next door.

So, like my dear friend Harry Dean Stanton, I went to Dan Tana's every night from 1971 through 1978, and like Norm on *Cheers*, we had both earned our seats at the bar there.

Michael, the bartender, always knew your drink when he spotted you at the door. So by the time you reached the bar, your beverage was ready and waiting.

Double vodka tonic, tall glass with a lime. And Michael poured a generous two-ounce double. So after a dozen or more of those, I'd be fairly enlightened.

Though some regulars might head home after dinner and a few drinks, Harry and I would always stay till last call, then head back to his place on Canyon Drive in the Hollywood Hills, where we'd watch movies on the Z Channel (a precursor to HBO) or simply leave the TV off and listen to a tape of Alan Watts.

After years of this, Harry and I got roles in the same movie, a first for us, and we were out of town for some time working with Warren Oates and Monte Hellman on *Cockfighter*. (If you think that title is about something other than battling birds, I'm sorry to disappoint you.)

At some point, it occurred to us that we had been gone for more than two weeks and should probably check in with Michael, to see if he and our friends at Tana's missed us.

Missed is an understatement. They had just dispatched someone to Harry's to peek in the window and see if we had fallen asleep with the gas turned on watching the Z Channel!

That was the only possible explanation for us being gone for fourteen days: death by asphyxiation. That, or a suicide pact between two lovers.

Look what I'm doing . . . this chapter was supposed to be about Alan Watts, and it morphed into a tale of Harry Dean, and now I'm dragging us into the Troubadour and Dan Tana's.

But the years I spent there are something of a miracle. How I did not accidentally kill myself, or someone else, is still a mystery to me, as my intake was not restricted to alcohol.

Pills, pot, coke, even four separate experiments snorting heroin, purchased at Tana's from Cathy Evelyn Smith, who administered the lethal dose to my dear friend John Belushi some years later.

I bristle when folks focus on drugs when they speak of the late great John Belushi . . . he was so much more than that. And I'd like to think I am, too.

But this is part of my story, as it was of John's, and it's important to note that John Belushi became my savior on more than one occasion when we did a movie together in 1977.

He and his wife Judy dragged me from the El Presidente Hotel in Durango, Mexico, because they couldn't bear to see me sit there and drink myself to death in the lobby bar.

Short recap: My consumption was such that it became a source of concern for John Belushi.

Because not only did I drink a quart of vodka nearly every day from 1971 through 1979, I also operated a vehicle.

While in Durango, I drove a car into a ditch, and John and I had to get the Mexican Teamsters to pull us out before Harold Schneider and Harry Gittes, the producers of the movie found out, or worse . . . the director and star, Jack Nicholson.

Of course, they already knew about it. They were the ones who sent the Teamsters to save the two gringos. Durango was a small town.

But back in L.A., I didn't always have such star power to bail me out of difficult spots I would get myself into, so I had to improvise when I was on my own.

One particular evening leaps to mind.

Christmas Eve, 1975.

It struck me as rather depressing that I should sit alone on Christmas Eve and self-administer my medicine. So I called up my friend Neil Rhodes, and he agreed to join me at Tana's, which was so much more festive than drinking at home. But let me not misrepresent Tana's as some sort of winter wonderland that year. They had a few strands of lights carelessly draped over the Chianti bottles that hung from the ceiling year-round. That was it.

So, having ingested about a quart of hard liquor, Neil proposed heading over to the Rainbow on Sunset, where he had heard tell of a proper Christmas party, already in full swing.

He heard right. As Neil and I arrived, we were immediately greeted by a sea of drunks in Santa hats. Frosty, the bartender, was wearing deer antlers and held up a bottle of Smirnoff, to see if we wanted our usual.

I'm not certain how anyone kept a straight face when I announced, "I better switch to white wine . . . I'm driving."

So switch I did, and soon consumed a quart of chardonnay to balance out the vodka. Then Frosty returned and offered me a mint from a small tin that he held, which I declined, slightly offended. I didn't remember eating any onions or garlic. But a quick assessment of my dietary choices for the day reminded me that I hadn't eaten *anything*.

But Frosty was still there, tin opened, rattling his mints and grinning.

"714, man," he finally offered, by way of explanation, glancing around furtively.

"I know," I said, thinking he was referring to the 714 area code. "These Orange County ladies are a little too conservative for my taste, but hot." When he jiggled the tin a bit closer, I finally realized he was not offering me a mint, but a Quaalude.

A Quaalude was a powerful hypnotic drug that I should have spotted right away, with the telltale 714 embossed on one side. It was time to fully recognize his generous offer but, in the interest of safety on the road . . . politely decline.

"Bless you, Frosty, my brother. You know I like my ludes, but I just drank a quart of vodka, a bottle of chardonnay, and I gotta get over Laurel Canyon . . . "

Who was I trying to kid? My heart wasn't in it.

"Y'know what . . . just give me a half," I offered, in a Solomon-like compromise.

Frosty obliged and broke off a half for me.

There were a good many safety instructions included with a prescription of Quaaludes. The top two were "Don't mix with alcohol" and "Don't operate machinery" . . . like a car.

But fifteen minutes and a few drinks later, I was feeling so good, so enlightened, that I motioned Frosty over. "Y'know what . . . can I grab another half?"

Fifteen minutes after that "Could I . . . ?" I pantomimed popping a pill and he slipped me another half, as someone else turned the lights on, signaling last call.

As Neil and I headed to the car, I was able to formulate a plan for what remained of Christmas.

I was in no shape to make it back to my place, so the question was:

Could I crash on Neil's couch and try to sleep this one off? Neil nodded in affirmation as we pulled onto Sunset from the parking lot.

I then asked the most important question of the night: "Do you have any liquor in your house?"

"Let's not take chances," responded Neil. "We'll stop at Greenblatt's and get something for the morning. We don't want to be caught short for Christmas Day."

Suddenly, I couldn't take my eyes off Neil. I had known Neil Rhodes since Van Nuys High. He was my best friend, my financial adviser, my drinking buddy. I looked at him and said, "I love you, man!"

But Neil got this weird look on his face, and I wondered if that had offended him somehow. It was only when he braced for impact that I remembered that I was driving a car and finally looked out the front windshield.

In an instant, there was metal and glass everywhere as I struck several vehicles that had stopped at the red light at San Vicente.

At this time, I was driving a Toyota Land Cruiser, and I will chart the tortured path from my electric car in 1970 to a small SUV in 1975 in a later chapter.

The first car I hit was an aging Ford LTD containing four very large African American gentlemen who were less than thrilled with me, as I had raked along the passenger side of their car, rendering those doors inoperable.

But even greater damage was suffered by the Honda Civic that I had hit so squarely from behind. Several hubcaps and other roundish parts continued to roll down San Vicente as I exited my car and prayed that the occupant was not injured or worse.

He was.

Injured, not dead. And somehow, not injured by me. He slowly extricated himself from the Honda holding a pair of crutches, with his left leg in a cast. I would later learn that he had been in a skiing accident and had just driven home from Big Bear.

In spite of all that damage to those two cars, I needed to focus my attention on a third vehicle stopped at the light . . . one I did not hit. The one that had two L.A. County sheriff's deputies in it. All of this having occurred just a few feet from their cruiser.

Keep in mind, I have consumed a quart of vodka, a bottle of chardonnay, a quaalude and a half in the last couple of hours . . . all on an empty stomach.

But as a result of the trouble I now found myself in, my veins were suddenly coursing with a new chemical compound that was counteracting the effects of all the drugs and alcohol: adrenaline.

I was, miraculously, not slurring my words as I shouted to the drivers I had just hit. "I'm so sorry! My fault! One hundred percent!" Then I turned to the deputies. "Gentlemen, sorry to mess up your Christmas, *everybody's* Christmas."

As one of the deputies went to check on the other drivers, the second deputy asked, "Did you not see the vehicles stopped at the light?"

"I've been pumping these brakes since back at Doheny . . . "

Unimpressed, he cut me off. "Can I see some ID, please?"

As I reached into the car and handed him my license, the first deputy returned. "Have you been drinking tonight, Mr. Begley?"

"Guys, it's Christmas Eve, I had a few drinks with friends, I live just two blocks from here . . . "

An obvious lie. My license said otherwise. But the fact that he hadn't clocked that made me go all in.

"You know what, guys . . . write it up any way you want. I'm rip-roaring drunk! Arrest me and take me in! It will probably only help my case when I sue the manufacturer of this piece of shit," I railed, now pointing at the car. "I've had it in three times this week to fix these defective brakes. I'm not joking, guys, I'm serious. Arrest me and take me in."

They seemed genuinely shocked by this approach and just stared at me for a bit.

But what happened next was truly shocking.

I had the deputies under the car with me inspecting the brake lines for leaks, pulling on the emergency brake to see if that was likewise damaged. It wasn't. None of it was. The only problem with the brakes was that I hadn't used them.

Not only did they not arrest me, they would soon let me get back in the car and drive home. Clearly, they hadn't seen the address of my license. I did *not* live two blocks away.

At some point in the confusion, I spotted the guy in the Honda Civic, the Crutches Guy, at a pay phone. He was trying to call a cab as the twisted wreckage of his car was being towed away, but I walked over and hung up the phone on him. "I can't have you pay for a cab. I'm the one responsible for this. I'll drive you home!"

But by the time all the paperwork was completed, my adrenal glands had been squeezed dry, and I was back to being pretty high.

At this point the Crutches Guy was really having second thoughts about getting in a car with me, especially one I earlier claimed had defective brakes, but I coerced him into the front seat with his crutches, and Neil climbed in back.

As I start to drive him home heading east on Sunset, I couldn't help but notice this loud metallic noise that my car had never made before: "Bam . . . bam-bam . . . bam."

"Does anyone know what that noise is?" I asked the Crutches Guy, but he remained silent and afraid. Neil quickly solved the mystery: "Yeah, you're way too close to the cars parked on the right. You're knocking the mirrors off. Correct to your left a bit."

As I attempted to make the adjustment, Crutches Guy had had enough. "Let me off here."

"No, I said I'd take you home and I am taking you home," I reasoned.

Crutches Guy, now scared for his life, finally bellowed, "Let me out of this car, you fucking psycho!" as he hit me in the face and chest with his crutch for emphasis.

I obliged and pulled over.

"Hobble home, then, ingrate!" was my parting shot, as he did indeed hobble while I resumed my trip to Neil's house.

We rode in silence for a bit till I remembered: "You think Greenblatt's is still open?"

But with all that had gone on that night, I remained completely unaware of what had really gone on with the deputies, or more precisely what had *not* gone on.

They had not arrested me and taken me in. Why was that?

Was it because I was a blond twenty-six-year-old who looked like them? Would they have afforded that same courtesy to others, let's say . . . to the four African American gentlemen in the LTD?

I suspect not.

For the first thirty years of my life, I was completely oblivious to my good fortune and my privilege. I hadn't a clue that I had won the lottery by being born Ed Begley's son and growing up in Merrick, then Van Nuys.

I saw myself as a victim of a Hollywood studio system that wasn't giving me the prime roles I deserved in a timely manner.

I had a "Wake me when I'm famous" attitude that kept me from putting in the kind of work required to land those plum parts, or the work necessary to achieve anything resembling spiritual awareness.

I had many lessons to learn, and several of them almost killed me before they woke me up.

How did I get to be that drunken maniac knocking the mirrors off parked cars in 1975?

The seeds were planted back at Valley College in 1968.

But not the leaves.

Those, we smoked.

The James Gang

I HAVE A GOOD MANY talented friends who were schooled back east, who attended Juilliard, Carnegie Mellon, and NYU. As well as many who attended prestigious California universities like UCLA or USC.

Not only did I not have the kind of dosh those schools required, I certainly hadn't the grades either.

I instead attended one of the many fine schools in the L.A. community college system. Referred to back then as "high school with ashtrays." (Yes, you could smoke in class back then, and yes, they had ashtrays at many of the desks on campus.)

It was there that I met my core group of college friends, and three of them are still among the living: Michael Richards, Neil Rhodes, and James Jeremias.

Let me start with Michael.

Michael Richards and I had a comedy act in the late sixties and early seventies. Then he wised up and went off on his own, did the hit comedy show *Fridays* for three years, then the megahit show *Seinfeld* for ten years and three Emmys.

Neil Rhodes and I met at Valley College but became close friends when I moved next door to him in 1971. He gave me the Alan Watts book *This Is It*, which changed my life for the better, and whatever small amount of fiscal responsibility I possess, I owe to Neil.

In 1971, he made around $4,000 working for BioScience Labs delivering blood samples, and somehow managed to saved $2,000 of it to travel the world. And not just Europe. He went to places like Kabul and Saigon in 1972, and he is the one who should be writing a book, not me.

James Jeremias and I became good friends in 1968 and remain so to this day. We enjoy a meal together at least once a week and talk on the phone often.

We met in Peter Gibbons's cinematography class at Valley College, which was one of the best bargains in higher education that I have ever known.

A class like that cost $24 a semester and was taught by a man who ran the camera department at CBS Studio Center, and also worked for George Stevens and other big names in cinema as a cameraman.

Pete was a great teacher. He would lecture occasionally but would regularly bring in camera equipment and other visual aids to make a point.

One day, when introducing us to the basics of film lighting, he arrived at class with not one but three identical slide projectors. Each was fitted with a different filter. He turned them on separately, and they were blue, green, and red.

But when he aligned the beams of light from each projector on a common screen, there was an absence of *any* color on said screen . . . just pure white light.

Then he walked forward and took a place in front of the screen. There were now blue, green, and red shadows, as well as yellow, magenta, and cyan in the overlap of those shadows.

He also introduced us to Ohm's law and other basic concepts that you need to know to operate camera motors and batteries.

I was a habitually bad student for most of my schooling prior to that. I loved science, but the nuns held little interest in that. The science that they did teach involved rising from the dead after three days and the resultant ascension to heaven, so when I got a good teacher, I learned to appreciate them.

Talk about a good use of our tax dollars. Thanks to the Los Angeles community college system, and $48 per annum on our end, James and I both wound up getting an education that got us into Hollywood craft unions. I worked as a camera assistant for years, and he got into Local 80 as a grip.

I also took acting and other theater arts classes, priced about the same as Pete's class, as did James, and we both moved on to even more lucrative careers in entertainment.

James enjoyed a successful writing career that included the eighties hit *Lost Boys*, For my part, I've been stumbling through a modest acting career for the past fifty-six years.

James and I have never really been out of touch, and he and his folks were always very good to me.

Before I got in the camera union or worked much as an actor, his mother Judy got me a job at an outfit in Van Nuys called Inspection Service. They did Zyglo, Magnaflux, and X-ray testing of parts, mostly for the aircraft industry.

They also did degreasing of parts. Parts that had just come off a lathe or milling machine were often coated in machine oil, and that oil needs to be removed.

It was a task often left to me that consisted of dipping pieces of metal in a large vat containing trichloroethylene, a toxic solvent (still present in the water table throughout the San Fernando and San Gabriel Valleys).

On a day that I had degreasing chores, I didn't need to sneak a joint behind the building to get high. It was built into the workday. Having a job at Inspection Service was huffing heaven, since this was 1968 and there was no OSHA, no overhead fan or mask requirement.

After about fifteen minutes of inhaling those fumes, the room was spinning and you needed to take a break. You'd head outside into the smog, as that was far better than what you were inhaling inside.

But it was a good-paying job for me, and I was grateful to have it. Until I slammed into a car on the 405 that had stopped suddenly, as did my paychecks. I was fired that same day. And who could blame them. The truck was destroyed, and the aircraft parts were all over the freeway.

Can you see a pattern emerging here?

"Do you know Ed Begley Jr.?"

"No, but I've run into him several times."

I drank rarely when I was back at Valley College. Back then, we all loved our pot and could not imagine watching a play, being in a play, watching a movie, being in a movie, going to the bank, going to the post office . . . anything, without firing up a joint first.

Long before alcohol put me in some dangerous situations, pot certainly did the trick.

I lived in Northridge. James lived in Chatsworth. So it was a short ride to visit his friend David Kurland, up an old road that led to Simi Valley.

Such was the time, we didn't find it unusual that David was living in a tree house next door to a saloon. He showed us some magnificent drawings he had done when he was shooting speed, but the work he'd done since he stopped was even better.

We smoked the one joint that we had brought with us, and then David suggested the family living just up the hill usually had pretty good dope.

We arrived at the family's house, and everyone looked pretty stoned already but welcomed their neighbor David and his two friends, me and James.

I didn't clock a lot of details at the time. It was the late sixties, so it was just another joint, shared with just another bunch of strangers, at a house I had never been to before, and to which I would probably never return.

We made small talk with them all, but only one of them recognized my name and knew who my father was. Apparently, he was a musician, and he was trying to get his music heard by someone in the business.

This was 1968, and I would not be onstage at the Troubadour for another year, so I didn't have a lot of contacts, but I told him I'd ask around and get back to him.

We said goodbye and returned to our car, still parked next to the tree house and the saloon.

I'm not sure if I mentioned earlier that the saloon was not a real saloon but part of a movie set on a western street at the Spahn Ranch.

Though I didn't get any of their names at the time, I would see and recognize several of them in the paper a year later.

Linda, Susan, Patricia, Tex, and especially the wannabe musician.

Charlie had something about him. Really hard to forget. I think it was his eyes.

If my friend Don McLean's song "American Pie" was about the day that Buddy Holly died, then August 9, 1969, was the day that hippiedom died. I had longish hair and dressed more nerd than flower child, but hitchhiking became a fairly futile effort after that. A small inconvenience for me. A much bigger burden for the families of Sharon Tate, Jay Sebring, the LaBiancas, and the other victims.

This would not be the last time where my addiction would place me in perilous situations with actual murderers. As I laid out in the first chapter, my addiction would begin with pills, then pot, then copious amounts of liquor, and other substances legal and illegal.

And even after that was all behind me, I had other addictive behavior waiting in the wings, ready to take a starring role.

222 Precious

AS THE DETAILS OF THE Tate–LaBianca murders came to light and the Manson family were brought to justice, I was working mostly as a camera assistant. Though I had gotten my first acting job in 1967 on a show called *My Three Sons*, my phone was somehow not getting the wear and tear that I had anticipated.

But this was not a total defeat. I loved camera work every bit as much as acting. And given the good training I received at Valley College, I applied for and got into the camera union, where I found consistent work as a camera technician on numerous commercials.

I was starting to pay my own way.

It was the proudest time I experienced with my father, and I'm so glad I had that before he passed a few years later, in 1970.

From what I've written so far, you might get the impression that I didn't much care for him, but such is not the case. The Mark Twain quote certainly applied to me: "When I was fourteen, my father was so ignorant, I could hardly stand to have the old man around. But when I got to be twenty-one, I was astonished at how much the old man had learned in seven years."

I would often complain about the smog, which was so bad back then, you couldn't go outside and play many days of the year. It seared your lungs.

But when I complained about it to my dad, he'd say: "I know what you're against . . . smog. I hate it too, but what are you *for*? What are you going to do about it? If you don't like smog, why don't you go build a clean car, or change the laws, or do something to make things better."

I had seriously never thought of that before. What a concept.

So when the first Earth Day was announced in 1970, I was primed and ready to do something. And there was much to do.

The Cuyahoga River outside Cleveland caught fire in 1969, and I thought that might also be a bad sign . . . rivers so polluted they catch fire . . . then the Santa Barbara oil spill off the California coast . . . you get the picture.

Lots of negatives to get you motivated.

But the positive influences motivated me even more. I was a Boy Scout, so I got to see nature up close and personal, and I felt it was worth protecting.

Topping that list of positives was my father. He was the son of Irish immigrants, and he had lived through the Great Depression. We turned off the lights, turned off the water, saved string and tinfoil.

It's probably widely known that I am a progressive. It is perhaps less widely known that my father was not.

We wound up on opposite sides of many issues, including the war in Vietnam, but I had to admire a man in his late sixties who went over to Southeast Asia and entertained the troops for an extended tour, visiting thousands of soldiers on shipboard and in hospitals. And I'm certain they all benefited from seeing his friendly and familiar face.

Though I had my challenges with my father, I loved him deeply.

I continued to work as a camera assistant, and I would occasionally get a day's work as an actor on *Adam-12* or *Mannix*, but I eventually got my first somewhat regular on-camera job on *Room 222*.

I certainly was not a *regular* regular on that fine show, but I did do about seven episodes, and oddly, my name changed with each episode that I was hired for. I was Bob, Willard, Stretch Webster, George, and Michael.

But at this point I had never been on more than one episode of anything. So after six episodes with the same cast and crew, something new happened for me as an actor:

I finally became relaxed in front of the camera.

And I thought I was home free, and consequently spent the next twelve years . . . being relaxed in front of the camera.

I suppose it was a step up from the nervousness I felt in my earlier work, but do you really want to watch a TV show, play, or movie where everyone is . . . relaxed?

I had much to learn, and fortunately this particular TV show would provide me with help in that department, too. Not only were the regular cast wonderful, but the guest cast included Richard Dreyfuss, Bruno Kirby, and Cindy Williams.

All of whom soon became close friends of mine but also inspired and educated me with their amazing work onstage and onscreen.

Let me start with Cindy, who we sadly lost this past year. Many remember her from *Laverne & Shirley*, but let's not forget that she also starred in George Lucas's *American Graffiti*, Francis Ford Coppola's *The Conversation*, and *Travels with My Aunt*, directed by George Cukor.

But this was long before that. I met her at the *Room 222* Christmas party, and I summoned the courage to ask her out on a date.

She was probably a bit thrown when I arrived in my electric car, a Taylor-Dunn, which I purchased in 1970 for $900 from a fellow named Dutch in Reseda.

When I say *car*, I'm being quite grand. It was basically a golf cart with a windshield wiper and a horn. Taylor-Dunn still makes electric cars to this day. Or, more precisely, electric *carts* to this day. I hadn't made that distinction back then.

In 1970, I took Cindy Williams on a date in my electric *cart*, and all I'll say is there was not a second date.

I hadn't correctly gauged the distance or the hills to and from the restaurant, and by the time we got there, the charge was so low, there was a kid passing us on a Big Wheel.

I loved Cindy Williams. I wanted to marry Cindy Williams.

Fortunately, for Cindy, she had the good judgment to never allow our relationship to become that, and we instead had a long and wonderful friendship that endured these past fifty-three years.

Cindy was godmother to my forty-five-year-old daughter Amanda, and I borrowed the money from Cindy to make the down payment on my first house.

Oh, shit. I've made a few bucks since then. Do you think her heirs will read this?

The truth is, I had to hound *her* to return the funds I had borrowed to buy that home. And, as fate would have it, the moment that escrow closed, my work dried up like the Aral Sea. It took me three years to pay her back in full! But when I brought up the matter of paying her interest (sky-high back then), she threw me out of her house.

Cindy treated me like a brother, and I am grateful beyond words to have had that place in her life these past fifty-three years.

And lest I mislead you, it was not merely her lack of romantic interest in me that placed me so squarely in the "brother" category. There was a far greater reason she spurned my many advances over the years: She was in love with another man. A man entirely worthy of her affections, and mine: Harry Gittes.

I had much cause to love Harry Gittes. It was he who introduced me to Jack Nicholson, Cass Elliot, Buck Henry, Helena Kallianiotes, Warren Beatty, and Michelle Phillips.

His house on Beverly Drive was a gathering place for so many bright and talented folks living in or visiting L.A. in the seventies. And they probably counted me in the visitor category, since I lived in the Valley.

But Harry welcomed me into the fold and later gave me a nice role in a film that his pal Jack Nicholson starred in and directed called *Goin' South*. The cast included me, Christopher Lloyd, John Belushi, and a newcomer named Mary Steenburgen.

I already mentioned my time in Durango on that film, and I surely will again, as it was another big leap forward in my growth as an actor, thanks to an able teacher named Jack who doesn't mince words.

Cell Service

THERE IS PROBABLY A MEDICAL name for it.

The condition where you tell a story a certain way for so long, you start to believe that it's actually the way things occurred.

It's surely a variant of me looking for my homework in Sister Killean's trash can, or O. J. searching for the real killer.

In my fantasy version of this particular evening, I am innocently walking the short distance from the Troubadour to Dan Tana's, where I had intended to grab a bite before my set.

But before I can make it to the front door of the restaurant, two L.A. sheriff's deputies descend on me and, lacking any rhyme or reason, arrest me for impersonating an officer. I sat in jail over the weekend, and then I was released late Monday on an O.R. (my own recognizance).

The truth is every bit as interesting as this fanciful tale. And it still culminates with me spending the weekend in County, and getting out on an O.R., but I must've figured the story needed a little more oomph back in 1972, lest it not be made clear what an innocent victim I was.

Let me attempt to tell the real story now, something I believe I've done so far in each of the previous chapters.

This story begins, not at the Troubadour, but at a small restaurant in Northridge where a friend, Carson Kievman, asked me to perform a short set while folks dined at this little hole in the wall, just south of Nordhoff on the east side of Reseda Boulevard.

I'm not sure if I knew the name of this venue in 1972, but I certainly don't know it now.

Carson was fond of my "cop routine," a piece that I regularly opened with, laden with drug humor that was always a crowd-pleaser in the early seventies.

Except when it wasn't.

I usually got nice laughs with this five-minute bit where I would have someone announce over the PA: "Our headliner will be out shortly, but prior to that, the management has agreed to let a member of the Los Angeles Police Department come onstage and say a few words . . . "

This would often anger the crowd, so much so that some would boo.

That was good news for me. Those who booed the loudest would soon be the ones laughing the hardest. The announcer was instructed to continue, no matter how vigorous the protest.

"Quiet down, please . . . he's here to say a few words about what has become a major problem in our schools, our homes, and the workplace: drug abuse. Welcome please, Officer Ed Begley!"

And onstage I came, in an actual LAPD uniform.

Fact check. Where does a civilian buy a real LAPD uniform in 1972?

Why, at Sam Cook Uniforms in downtown L.A. Where the actual cops and firefighters bought their uniforms back then. And still do today.

I purchased the official pants and shirt, the official belt and holster, complete with a handcuff caddy, a flashlight loop, and one of those little stainless name tags that simply said, "Begley."

Badges were a different story, of course, and since an LAPD shield was unavailable to me, I picked up one that simply said "Special Police." People rarely look closely at badges.

But there were shoulder patches for sale that reflected the different divisions. I picked up a pair that announced to the world that I was part of the Motor Division.

And it certainly looked like I was in the Motor Division when I pulled up in a black-and-white police car that I would get for special occasions.

Yes, a mere civilian could get their hands on a black-and-white police car, if you agreed to mention the Ford Motor Company in the end credits of your film.

I had little interest in buying a police car, but I did buy the entire police outfit in 1972, and the most important thing to note is . . . I can still fit into it today.

Okay, that's actually not the most important thing (though it is true!). The most important thing to note is how clueless I was about basic stagecraft.

This bit killed that night on Reseda Boulevard. It killed at the Troubadour. The Comedy Store, the Ice House, the Bottom Line, Max's Kansas City, and countless other clubs big and small across America.

Where it did *not* kill was at Nassau Coliseum in 1974, when I opened for Poco, John Sebastian, and Loggins and Messina.

The crowd in attendance might have liked my set, but we'll never know, owing to a major lapse in judgment on my part. Did I mention that I was a prop comic?

The LAPD uniform was just the first in a series of costumes and props that I would employ over the course of an evening. And that uniform and others were fitted with Velcro for quick removal behind a changing screen I had behind me onstage.

Some additional props included a nun's habit, an IV stand, a ventriloquist's dummy, and a large magician's American flag that seemed to appear out of nowhere.

I have audio recordings of this ridiculous act, but I'm quite grateful that there is no video of it.

Back to the Nassau Coliseum, where the crowd *loved* it.

Well, the first ten rows did.

But since there were 18,000 people in attendance, and since there were no jumbotrons in 1974, the other 17,800 people *could not see* the

16-by-20 photographs that I was holding up as visual punch lines to my spiel.

Basic stagecraft.

I wised up a short time later and increased the size of my imagery when I played a large venue. Who knew that Carrot Top and Gallagher would become role models for me in the sophisticated genre of prop comic?

But not being able to see my props from a distance was a problem long before that night at Nassau Coliseum.

Especially the night that began this chapter. The one where I was arrested outside the Troubadour in 1973.

Before there was a West Hollywood, the neighborhood around the Troubadour fell under the jurisdiction of Los Angeles County, and police enforcement in that vicinity was carried out not by LAPD but by the Los Angeles County Sheriff's Department.

So when two sheriff's deputies sitting across the street from the Troubadour saw me exit on my way to Tana's, they thought I was a real LAPD officer and quickly exited their vehicle to gain some clarity as to why I was in their jurisdiction.

"Are you in pursuit?" one of them called out as they approached. I wasn't sure at first what that meant, but I soon realized, like that night at Nassau Coliseum, they couldn't see my props from a distance, or lack thereof.

I had taken off my badge and my toy gun, belt, and holster. I thought I looked like a security guard on the way to work. But from across that very wide stretch of Santa Monica Boulevard (a train still ran down the middle in the seventies), I must've looked like a cop to them.

They claimed it was the shoulder patches that had gotten their attention and crossed the line into "impersonating an officer" territory. I pleaded my case, explaining that I was just an actor about to go onstage at the Troubadour.

Not quite true. I was an actor, and I had been onstage that evening in that cop costume, but not anywhere around where we stood.

The only thing that I was doing at the Troubadour that night was drinking at the bar.

I had no booking to go onstage and perform there. That was all baloney, served up cold to a couple of sheriff's deputies, in hopes of getting off for the stupidity of wearing any remnant of law enforcement garb.

And there was an easy fix, when you think about it. I had all my costumes fitted with Velcro, remember? All I had to do was rip the top off, and suddenly I'm a guy in a T-shirt and black pants!

As a result of that poor judgment, I was cuffed and driven to the sheriff's station on San Vicente, where I was charged with impersonating an officer, a fairly serious crime then, as today.

One that dictated posting of bail in the amount of $500.

An impossible amount to put your hands on in 1973. There were no ATMs back then, and it was late on a Friday. There would be no banks open the next day, or the one that followed.

This was my first time in the San Vicente tank, and my cellmates were mostly drunks, which miraculously I *was not* on that evening. I had probably had a beer or two before being arrested, and that amount would surely not trigger the more lenient blood-alcohol threshold of 1972.

But I soon found myself wishing I had been drunk, as it would have been easier to tune out the snoring and off-gassing coming from my cellmates and get some shut-eye during this, my very first night in jail.

I was also soon reminded of the three basic necessities for survival. Food, shelter, and clothing.

Food was provided courtesy of Norms Restaurant on La Cienega. Cold as ice, and absent so much as a gram of plant matter.

The sheriff's station was certainly a well-fortified shelter.

My most pressing problem involved clothing.

All the other prisoners were allowed to stay in their civvies, but my clothing had been taken from me upon arrival, and placed securely in the evidence locker. So I was a bit concerned about sending the wrong signal to my cellmates: a twenty-two-year-old blond sitting there in my underwear.

I would remain in that tank for another eight hours. At which point the four of us who had not posted bail were loaded in a van and taken to the county jail in downtown L.A.

It is at this point that things get fairly serious.

This is no longer a holding tank where a drunk might sleep it off and be released, either by making bail or by eventually reaching a lowered blood-alcohol level.

This is County, the place where murderers, violent sex offenders, and other felons are housed till they await trial and are either released or transferred to Atascadero, Folsom, or some other federal penitentiary.

Due to the overcrowding in the jail back then (same as today), I was assigned to a cell with four bunk beds . . . along with four other guys. It quickly became clear that one of us was sleeping on the floor.

I got lucky and wound up in a bunk.

The last cellmate arrived long after me, in a seriously intoxicated state, and had no problem sleeping on the floor.

At the other end of the spectrum, there was a gentleman accepted by all to be the alpha male in our cell. He was an extremely large and fit African American gentleman whose name I somehow do not recall, but for the purposes of this chapter, let's call him Alfie.

The first thing Alfie asked me when I arrived was "What's your beef?"

We were just getting to know each other, so it was understandable that he was not aware of my dietary restrictions, but if he was taking dinner orders, I told him to "put me down for the lentil loaf."

This risky exchange worked out quite well for me, actually, as it pointed out a currency that I possessed that I was not even aware of.

I made Alfie laugh . . . heartily.

And that proved to be an extremely valuable commodity that I traded successfully during my three days in Cell Block B. It made the time pass more quickly for all of us.

I had been doing stand-up for about four years at this point, but for this weekend gig at L.A. County, I did some of my best work. Think

Donald O'Connor and the musical number "Make 'Em Laugh." Subtitled "And Keep Their Mind off Other Things."

And I quickly learned that the "What's your beef?" query had nothing to do with food.

Your "beef" was your crime.

Alfie's beef was manslaughter. A horrible charge in most settings, but in a cell at County, it was considered prime beef.

Impersonating an officer was more like beef jerky.

"Why were you impersonating a cop?" was the obvious question that Alfie got to quickly.

I then fabricated an elaborate tale about showing up at a drug deal dressed as a cop and making off with contraband and cash.

He stared at me long and hard after that disclosure, then broke into an even heartier laugh, thinking I was trying to entertain him again. I went with it, and later told him some version of the truth.

Though Alfie had disclosed that his beef was manslaughter, he never really gave any details. Whatever the case, Alfie turned out to be my best audience and my greatest ally during my three days in jail.

No one bothered me during my entire time there, because of my friendship with him.

Monday morning came quickly, and I was transported by bus to the Beverly Hills courthouse, where I was assigned a public defender. He seemed quite surprised with my story (the true one) and vowed to get me out on my own recognizance that same day, and did.

I was sent back to the county jail to gather my belongings, and I did.

But before I was released into the night in downtown L.A., I asked for a visit with an inmate named Alfie and gave him everything I had on me.

I didn't have a lot of money to give him, but he was grateful for what little I had. Simple things like a cloth handkerchief or a pack of mints have tremendous value to someone on the inside.

I prevailed in court a few weeks later, and all charges were dropped. The public defender even made them return my police uniform . . . after removing the Motor Division patches.

At the end of the day, my privilege got me out of jail unharmed, and quickly. But not before I saw the stark reality of who made up the prison population in Los Angeles, and how much harder it was for them to find justice.

It planted a seed that later took hold and motivated me to try to change that very flawed system.

Years later, I would meet and eventually work with Desmond Tutu, a man who had a great deal of experience trying to reform the prison system in Africa and around the world.

With his courage and commitment, we saw the end of apartheid in 1994. Would we see meaningful prison reform and social justice here in America anytime soon?

It would prove more difficult than any of us imagined.

Breakfast of Champions

RIGHTLY OR WRONGLY, THERE ARE a good many folks who associate me with healthy living, and quite specifically healthy eating, so this might be a good time for me to explain some of my dietary choices over the years.

I stopped eating beef in 1970 after the first Earth Day and after I watched my first slaughterhouse film. In that same year, I also stopped eating lamb, veal, pork, chicken, and all manner of birds, venison, and other game animals. I was a vegetarian at first, then became a vegan in 1992.

I personally feel it's better for my health, the health of the planet, and of course the animals in the cages.

I knew very little about cooking in those early days, but I now make at least thirty different appetizers, soups, salads, and entrées, all warmly praised by vegans and meat eaters alike. All incredibly delicious, and 100 percent vegan. So one can cultivate a regimen of a tasty vegan diet, if you're of a mind. And I don't always stay home and cook. I also love to eat out.

And when I had the resources to dine out during the seventies, I often found myself at the Old World Restaurant on Sunset near Tower Records, as I was drawn there by the vast array of organic vegetarian fare that they had available early in the a.m.

I should probably mention that they also had a full bar open at that hour, for those who were in need of a little medication with their muesli.

I became something of a regular there, and the following scene would eventually play out between me and every member of the waitstaff:

"Had a chance to look at the menu?" the server said as he approached.

"I have . . . Kevin," I said, clocking his name tag. "And I have a couple questions: the Belgian waffle? Is that made with 100 percent organic whole wheat flour?"

"It is," he said, emboldened by my attention to detail. "As well as Alta Dena organic raw milk and butter."

Uh-huh. "The eggs?"

"Organic and cage free, from Shelton Farms," he said proudly.

"Okay, then. I'll have the waffle and a couple of eggs, scrambled . . . and . . . " as if it had just occurred to me, "is the bar open at this hour?"

"The bartender's setting up right now." Kevin seemed as proud of this as he was with their alliance with Shelton Farms.

Good. "Bring me a couple of Bloody Marys while you're at it."

"Right away," said Kevin as I handed him back his menu, allowing me to settle in on my other morning ritual, the crossword.

And that's when I spotted it. Seventeen across. "PTL televangelist" was the clue.

He was new on the scene, but I had heard of him. Jim Bakker. With two *K*s. And at nine letters, it fit nicely.

But wasn't it funny that this PTL guy had the same name as the former owner of the very restaurant where I was doing said crossword.

Jim Baker.

His legal name, spelled with the more common single "k," was James E. Baker, but he was known more recently as "Father Yod," who opened the Source Restaurant after his Old World investors fired him for stealing enough from the till to buy himself a Rolls-Royce, and for shooting a customer there.

And when I say *customer*, I really mean the irate husband of actress

Jean Ingram, who came in to the restaurant to confront him about the affair Jim was having with his wife.

Which proved to be a bad idea, as Jim quickly dispatched him with a karate chop and a bullet. Dispatched, as in dead.

I'd return to those thoughts and my crossword momentarily, but I noticed out of the corner of my eye that the two Bloody Marys that I had ordered had just landed beside me.

Relief was on its way. I picked up a glass and drank deeply only to notice there was only one red beverage at my side, not the two I had so clearly requested. I finished it quickly and searched frantically for Kevin.

Fortunately, my trembling raised hand soon got Kevin's attention, and he approached, explaining, "Your order's in. Should be ready in a few minutes."

"No rush on the food, but . . . maybe I wasn't clear with my drink order. I was hoping to get *two* Bloody Marys to start with, and . . . "

"Are you expecting someone? I'll get another place setting." And I had to nearly grab him to keep him from leaving on the wrong errand.

"I'm dining alone, actually, but I'd love to get to both of those drinks, and quickly, so if you could . . . "

I could see that Kevin was a bit confused by this order of two strong vodka drinks at eight a.m. for just one person, so I came at it from a slightly different angle.

"Here's the problem, Kevin. You're thinking like a waiter . . . understandable! You are a waiter. But for the purposes of my beverage order today, you are more of an air traffic controller."

Kevin was starting to look a little lost, so I picked up my drink glass to offer a visual aid.

"You got a flight taking off on runway 25-right at LAX." The plane *took off* from my table and *landed* at my mouth.

I then picked up my water glass and had it land at the "adjacent runway" on the other side of my place setting. "You want to have one landing at the same time on runway 25-left. You always want equipment on the ground."

There were surely many ways that he could have reacted to that little demonstration. He chose the one that he reasoned would best enhance his gratuity.

"I'll get right on it."

I returned to my crossword, but I couldn't stop thinking of our West Coast Jim Baker.

The one who got booted from this very restaurant, the Old World, to open the Source Restaurant, just down the street, where everybody who worked there wore white.

And when I say white, I mean all white. And when I say worked there, I mean they worked there, they just didn't get paid to work there.

Jim's new identity as "Father Yod" was part of a cult that he ran in the Hollywood Hills for many years.

To join the cult, you had to sign over all cash, trust funds, cars, and jewelry to the "Family." And for that valuable consideration you would be permitted to cook or wait tables at the Source. Or perform similar chores at Father Yod's estate in the hills above Sunset Boulevard.

At some point things got too dangerous for the Family in the L.A. area, as they had coerced a good many sons and daughters, wives and husbands into the cult, so they all moved to Hawaii, where Jim took up hang gliding and, without so much as an hour of training, plummeted to his death off a 1,300-foot cliff.

The entire family was convinced that their "Father" was still very much alive and would return to care for them after a brief visit to "the other side."

Though that of course never happened, I likewise waited patiently for Kevin to return from the other side of the restaurant where the bar sat, and had much better luck than our friends in Hawaii.

Kevin came back quickly with my food and two Bloody Marys, pointing to one of them and announcing: "No charge on this one. Sorry for the confusion." Then he retreated through the swinging doors of the kitchen, likely to stuff a napkin in his mouth to keep me from hearing the laughter he had somehow been able to contain in my presence.

It never occurred to me that there was anything contradictory about my strict rules on diet and my daily intake of alcohol, pills, and cocaine.

I would get up in the middle of a perfectly good bender with my drinking buddies and announce my departure, which would often elicit a "Where the fuck you think you're going?"

Straight-faced, I would explain, "I'm headed to the gym for a workout and a sauna. Then some brown rice and veggies. Wanna come?"

Unlike Kevin, my pub pals made no attempt to conceal their laughter and their disdain as they continued to seek nutrition from the pickled eggs and the pepperoni sticks that they found more palatable than what I was offering.

A savvy reader might take note of the proximity of the Old World, where Jim Baker had gotten away with murder, to a spot just a hundred yards away, where I was let off for drunk driving on Christmas Eve that could have easily gotten someone killed.

And, like Jim, because of the way I looked, I got off lightly.

But I had no appetite for dwelling on white privilege on this particular morning.

I had a hot meal on the table before me, a crossword to finish, and more drinks on the way.

Brave Men Run in My Family

AROUND THE SAME TIME I muscled my way into Harry Gittes's coterie of prestigious friends in the film business, I formed another life-long friendship with an icon in the L.A. art scene, Mr. Ed Ruscha, who has a famous artwork with the same title as this chapter.

It began innocently enough at my bungalow in the Valley when Paul Ruscha arrived with his brother Ed, who was experiencing his very first acid trip.

Paul reasoned that my design motif at the time, which was "Lapsed Catholic Chic," might enhance the experience, and he guessed right.

I would soon learn that the Ruscha lads and I had much in common, and it was a bromance at first sight. The problem with me, though, is that I don't know when to quit.

I already had them with my antique prie-dieu, a large portrait of the pope, and lots of votive candles. But in the presence of an artist of his stature, I chose to raise the stakes and change it up a bit.

As in a wardrobe change. Into my LAPD uniform.

What is truly amazing is that he remained not only calm but quite amiable in the face of this incongruous shift. He couldn't stop laughing.

In fairly short order, I became close friends with the talented Ruscha brothers, and eventually Ed's beautiful and brilliant wife Danna as well.

Ed and Danna had taken a decade-long hiatus from their first marriage together. But they couldn't stay apart forever. They had much in common creatively, and even more importantly, they were blessed with an amazing son, Eddie, who I have known since his single digits.

At some point during that pause, Danna and I became pals, and along with our mutual friend (and former go-go dancer at the Whisky) De De Mollner, we took an extremely memorable and fun trip to Billings, Montana, and camped out all along the way.

We intended to pay a visit to some friends who were filming a movie there called *The Missouri Breaks*.

The cast list included Jack Nicholson, Marlon Brando, Harry Dean Stanton, Fred Forrest, and Randy Quaid.

I wound up staying for a whole week and camped out on the banks of the Yellowstone River, then socialized on set and elsewhere till I had to return to L.A. for a film that I was actually in.

Which was *Stay Hungry*, which I would film that same year in Birmingham, Alabama.

Which I got through my friendship with Harry Gittes.

Which Harry felt comfortable recommending me for because he heard that I was just up in Montana with Jack.

And I must be on the approved list if Jack is granting me hang time in his trailer in Montana.

All based on pure chutzpah on my part.

I wound up getting evicted from my bungalow in the Valley around this time, and moving to . . . parts unknown.

I was starting to get booked at clubs around the country as an opening act, so I didn't need to have a permanent base for much of that year.

I was quite content to live in my car, or crash at my manager Herb Gart's place in Midtown Manhattan, or bully my way onto Paul Ruscha's couch at the Ruscha studios, then located on Western Ave., and I wound up staying . . . for the next decade.

Paul and Ed's generosity with an available couch was most gracious, but I should probably clarify that I didn't commandeer that spot for much more than a few weeks.

There was a lovely British couple, by the names of Jonathan Heale and Leslie Sunderland, who rented a studio in the Ruscha Courtyard for an amazing $75 a month.

Good rent even back then.

They needed to get back to Wales, as they also had a long and lasting friendship with actress Julie Christie, and they were caretakers on her property when she was off doing a movie, which was a great deal of the time.

They soon offered me an opportunity to sublet their L.A. space, and I did. I lived there, I worked there, I had my wedding party there in 1976.

I might mention that I was born just a few blocks away at Hollywood Presbyterian Hospital at Vermont and Sunset. Do humans return to their spawning grounds? I spent a good many years at the Ruscha complex, and some of my most creative.

Which I'm convinced occurred by being in close proximity to all manner of Ruschas.

Ed, if the couch isn't available, I'd be open to living nearby in my car. My current electric vehicle is quite comfortable.

Trash Talk

SOME VISITORS FROM OUT OF town wondered if we had taken up pottery, as the mysterious object in our yard certainly did look like a kiln. But if you were raised in Los Angeles, you knew what it was . . . a backyard incinerator. And, if you had one, you only needed two trash bins at the curb.

One for bottles and cans. And a second bin for wet waste, food scraps, and the like.

Then all the dry waste was incinerated in our backyard and eventually hauled away as ash. Much lighter and lower in volume, so it saved on space and hauling costs.

But as the sources of smog in Los Angeles became more quantifiable with more accurate studies, the environmental cost of burning all that trash started to cause some concern.

So, after power plants and mobile sources (cars and trucks), incinerators had become subject to regulation, then eventually removal in 1957.

I myself became very interested in trash about eight years later, when there was a renewed push for "no-deposit, no-return" bottles in America and elsewhere.

A good way to get a person's attention is to affect their pocketbook, for better or worse, and this was definitely worse, as the removal of the bottle deposit on beverages took money straight out of my wallet.

A single-serving beer or beverage bottle would redeem at the market for two cents, while the larger quart bottle would fetch a full nickel.

A bicycle basket filled with spent bottles could net you more than a dollar, and in the midsixties, a dollar was a threshold amount that still got your attention.

So I began to actually look at our weekly trash and consider where it all came from and where it would eventually go.

I performed a very primitive assessment of our consumption and was shocked by all the waste that we were responsible for.

Years later, my dear friend Annie Leonard would do a brilliant piece on this subject with *The Story of Stuff.*

The epiphany that occurred as a result of my lost deposit revenue made me start recycling (again!) in 1970 as part of my full commitment to Earth Day and all the activism that accompanied it.

Even though there was no CRV (California Redemption Value) on bottles or cans in the seventies and most of the eighties, I still drove my electric car and often rode my bike to the only recycling yard in the San Fernando Valley, located in Sun Valley, where they would accept your newspapers, bottles, and cans from noon to three p.m. on Saturday and Sunday.

As we now know, there have been a few missteps along the way with our well-intentioned desire to recycle. Specifically with plastics. It turns out that only a small percentage of it actually gets recycled.

A huge amount of it winds up in our oceans, in our rivers and streams and in our bodies. The best way we can have the most impact on plastic pollution is to stop all single-use plastic now.

Fortunately, I used very little plastic anyway before learning all this, and I was always fairly vocal about trash.

In the early nineties, I took part in an effort to stop expansion of the Sunshine Canyon Landfill in the San Fernando Valley, and I suggested to the county board of supervisors that we didn't really need more landfill space, if we did it right.

"A week's worth of trash in my household would probably fit in my glove compartment," I bragged at that same meeting.

The very next day, there was a lady at my door who identified herself as Tracey Kaplan from the *Los Angeles Times*. I thanked her but explained that I already took the paper.

She further clarified that she was a writer for the *Times* and had taken note of my claim that I could fit a week's worth of my trash in my glove compartment, at which point I had to confess that I had never actually done that, but I quickly added that it seemed to be an amount that modest.

She was then joined by her photographer, and I tried to appear pleased that I would get a fair assessment of my waste, as this was a Tuesday, and the trash pickup in Studio City is on Wednesday morning.

She was quite thorough about going room to room, and we soon had it all gathered in my garage, and it was only then that I realized how small the glove compartment is in a VW Rabbit.

A great car, converted from diesel to electric by my friend Richard Mayer, but I was starting to worry about how I was going to fit even my modest amount of trash in a space that might be able to accommodate one Birkenstock, but not two.

But I was ready for the challenge. I had just returned from a bike ride, so I was still in my bike shorts.

To get the trash to fit in my glove box, I had to use those biking quads to my full advantage. In fairly short order, we all heard the telltale click on the latch that signaled success.

A picture of me at that moment sat below the title of her funny and fair take on the whole story. It read "Actor Crams for Test."

But sadly, not all my trash talk has had a happy ending.

Back in 1974, the contents of my bin had become so malodorous that it prompted my neighbor across the alley (near Vineland and Ventura) to knock on my gate and ask if my cat had gone missing. She was afraid that it had gotten stuck under the house and died.

Before I could answer, tangible purring proof of my cat's well-being was rubbing up against my leg, but it soon became obvious that *something* had died nearby.

After a bit more olfactory analysis, I reasoned that it was a dead rat, as I had just come upon one in the attic of my manager Herb Gart's home, and the smell was identical.

By then, my neighbor had opened up my metal can, which revealed several large Hefty bags and a stench that was so overpowering, she quickly closed it back up, lest we both start to blow chunks.

"No, that's bigger than a dozen rats," I now theorized. "Someone must've put a dead dog in there, maybe got hit by a car."

My neighbor was now in full retreat. "I'll call animal control."

"Thank you! I'll be back in an hour, if you need me."

I had gotten on my bike and was happy to quickly be in the wind with that horrible smell behind me.

I was gone scarcely an hour and was prepared to tell what little I knew to the folks at animal control, but passage to my alley was now blocked by any number of black-and-white police cars, detective cars, and even a couple of police photographers.

I saw the flash go off a few times, so I knew they were taking pictures of something, but I couldn't make out what it was.

With my alley blocked, I was forced to walk my bike through my front gate and noticed an officer in my backyard.

"Hi. Do you live here?" he asked.

"11059½ Fruitland. Yes, this is my place. Is everything okay?"

"Just investigating a crime scene," he offered. "Have you seen anything unusual in your alley recently? Someone using your trash can that you hadn't seen before?"

During all this I was slowly making my way to the alley fence to see what was out there that was now producing a smell that was unbearable.

"Sir! Could you stand back from the fence. Anything unusual in the alley, that you might have seen or heard?"

I moved away from the fence and answered honestly. "No, nothing."

Seeing I had little to offer, he left a card on a backyard table and returned to the alley, glancing back at me to make sure I stayed away as he had asked me to.

Undeterred, I climbed up on my roof and tried to make out what they were all looking at and photographing. The six items that were now laid out like an exploded diagram.

The denial is so strong the first time you see something like this. I'm staring at it all, and I was still thinking, "Is that a large leather ottoman, surrounded by some smaller pillows, laid out beside it?"

Till the penny finally dropped, and I could clearly see that it was a torso, a head, two arms, and two legs.

Human remains, somehow left in my trash can.

Probably because there was a lot of room available.

A mess that was once a person. And now it was this.

Life and death are both undeniable, and inevitable.

One prepares you for the next. And it always will.

I would learn months later from an article in the *Times* that it was a young lady only fifteen years of age.

What had occurred in that child's short life that took her from her mother's arms to a stranger's trash can in an alley? And that filled me with a sadness I had not yet known.

But I was soon able to find some light among all that darkness of that grim discovery.

I could use it as another reason to drink.

He Devil

I PROBABLY BROKE A FEW hearts with my bad behavior in the eighties.

Including mine. That level of dishonesty doesn't work for anyone, including the perpetrator.

And let me be clear, my bad behavior was not restricted to just that decade. It was in full swing throughout the seventies and it kept apace till I finally grew up in 1996.

When I say I grew up, I mean that I was finally capable of being in a fully committed relationship . . . with one person at a time.

If you want multiple partners, I suppose that's fine (who am I to judge), but you should probably make that clear to your wife or girlfriend.

In my first marriage, I definitely wanted to become monogamous, but in my delusion, I actually thought that the act of putting a ring on my finger would make me monogamous. Turns out there's more to it than that.

Not that I had the best of role models. Let's not forget the trip to the DMV when I was fifteen, where I discovered that my father was having children with one woman while being married to another. He regularly had visits on set and backstage from his many "nieces."

Unless I'm missing a huge branch of the Begley family tree, my dad had a sum total of one niece. Both Jack Klugman and Tony Randall verified my father's antics over the years.

But let me return to *my* long list of dishonest behavior. Behavior that started not long after my first amorous interlude, which occurred rather late for me.

Late for anyone. I was twenty.

I was such an awkward nerd at the time, I must have emitted some sort of anti-pheromone because I somehow managed to *not* get laid in the sixties.

In a theater arts department.

In Los Angeles.

Old pictures of me and my apartment at the time hold a few clues.

I wore all white. Not ashram all white. Sears work clothes all white.

In lieu of Janis or Jimi posters, my walls held . . . pictures of various 16mm and 35mm cameras. The Mitchell BNC. The Éclair NPR. An Arriflex IIC.

My apartment reeked of Lysol, which was, for me, aromatherapy. Not so much for those who carry two X chromosomes.

But I had the extreme good fortune of having a lady friend who was gay. And this dear friend was aware of my situation, and she came to my apartment with her girlfriend one magic night in 1970 and bestowed on me a kindness I won't soon forget.

I have no delusions as to how lucky I am that two friends made that milestone in a young man's life so loving and tender.

But whatever brief gratitude I felt after that night did not last long. My father had passed away earlier that year, and perhaps because of his influence, I had trouble with honesty in my relationships.

In spite of that, I have come to know and be close to some of the most amazing, talented, and brilliant women of our time, and was even married to two of them.

In one case, I still am.

And it only took me twenty-six years to learn how to be a worthy husband or partner.

With many missteps along the way, especially when I got a small dose of fame back in 1976.

I had been an actor for nearly a decade when I finally got a role that briefly made me, if not a name actor, possibly a name-ette.

That show was called *Mary Hartman, Mary Hartman*. It was produced by Norman Lear and starred Louise Lasser and Mary Kay Place.

Part of my brief success in playing the character of Steve was that I finally gave the viewers what they probably wanted from me all along: I did not talk.

I hadn't so much as a line of dialogue in any of the episodes. The message was clear: "Just shut the hell up and you might work again in this business." That the character of Steve was also deaf might have also had something to do with it.

What happened next was quite surprising. While shooting this show at KTLA in Hollywood, I decided to swing for the fences and make a pitch for a woman who was clearly above my station . . . one Mary Kay Place.

Mary Kay was not only the extremely popular co-star of the show with Louise and others, she had already gotten great acclaim for writing an episode of *M*A*S*H* and appearing in it. She also released a hit country album.

After various forms of trickery and misrepresentation, I managed to get Mary Kay to go out with me, and we dated for the better part of a year.

I went to Tulsa to meet her folks, Brad and Gwen, as well as traveling to Rule, Texas, to meet her namesake and grandmother Mary.

But this was 1976, and I was at full throttle with my alcoholism, so rigorous honesty would elude me until I got sober, years later. The occasional sleepovers at the home of Groucho Marx that I referred to in the first chapter involved a lady other than Mary Kay.

I was very good friends with the great Tom Waits during those years, and his amazing album *The Heart of Saturday Night* was the theme music for my time with Mary Kay, and it proved an elixir through the sad times after we split up.

And Tom's friendship and artistic influence over the years has been an inspiration like no other in my life. Seeing him do the highest level of work as a songwriter *and* as an actor somehow even made a stiff like me reach even higher, and occasionally succeed.

His inspired collaboration with his wife Kathleen offers guidance for all couples who are lucky enough to work together.

So it was entirely apropos that Tom Waits and I were together when I met the woman who would soon be my wife.

It was a day like many other days for Tom and me in Los Angeles. We would start at Jack's Bar in downtown L.A. near 5th and Main, where well drinks were under a dollar.

Then, time and budgetary constrictions permitting, we would sometimes venture to Dan Tana's, if I had gotten a residual check or Tom had heard from ASCAP.

This was one of those lucky days, as I got a check for *Baretta*, *Mannix*, or another such epic I had done in the seventies. Mailbox money was always cause for celebration, so I convinced Tom that we should head west to Santa Monica and Doheny and the target-rich environment that the Troubadour and Dan Tana's afforded.

To seal the deal, I added, "You are not paying for a single drink tonight!"

We arrived at Tana's and I ordered a couple of beers. As I walked over to hand one to Tom, I saw that he was engaged in conversation with an attractive blonde. I gently passed Tom his beer, so as not to break his rhythm, but my stealth mode was somehow still distracting to the blonde, and she quickly chided me with "Excuse me . . . we're talking here."

I apologized briefly and backed away so as not to disrupt any further.

I think a full thirty minutes went by before I noticed that Tom was in need of a refill, so I ordered another and brought it down to him, as he was still chatting with the anonymous lady.

I know what you're thinking. Why didn't I just tell the bartender to bring Tom a beer?

I was clearly looking for trouble, and quickly found it. As I brought

Tom his refill, she sized me up and remarked, "I asked you to leave us alone and here you are again."

She was fairly well oiled by now, so she went so far as to physically push me away while explaining, "We're talking about Napoleon!"

I had no idea what that meant, but what happened next defied the laws of physics. In the act of pushing me away, she ripped open the antique shirt I was wearing. A shirt given me by the writer Eve Babitz, who I met at that very spot back at the bar in 1971 and wound up dating, on and off, for years.

But back to tonight's blonde. She was pushing me away, not pulling me toward her. I still don't know how that caused all the buttons to come off.

But I was now officially topless and upset with this lady, while Tom, for his part, was finding it all quite amusing.

Just as things were getting heated, my friend Mimi Machu came up and brokered a peace. A détente that miraculously involved us all sitting at a table together.

Mimi was somehow also able to find a few paper clips, which provided a temporary fix for the torn shirt, and things cooled down enough for me to get the blonde's name:

Ingrid.

But they didn't stay cooled down, since from this new angle right next to her . . . I could see she was *very* attractive.

The four of us sat together for the next hour or so. Margaritas were ordered, then more margaritas, then more still.

Eventually I learned what "We're talking about Napoleon" meant. Napoleon Lascaro was the fellow who did the cover art for *The Heart of Saturday Night*. I turned on the charm.

"I *love* that cover! Airbrush, right?"

Ingrid: [crickets]

I learned that she worked at the Tiffany Theater on Sunset Boulevard.

"The improv group . . . the Committee! . . . Do you know Carl Gottlieb?"

Ingrid: No longer crickets. Now centipedes.

Finally weary of my vain attempts at connecting with her, she whispered something in Mimi's ear and announced: "This has been fun, but us girls gotta run, but here's for our share of the tab."

And she lays a fin on the table.

Five dollars.

The two of them had just consumed their body weight in tequila, and then there's the business of the antique shirt . . . and all I could do was laugh and announce: "You are paid in full. The shirt, the drinks, in fact, can I validate your parking? You are good to go, let's just make each other one promise . . . we will never speak again."

She seemed to look right through me when she said: "That won't be a problem."

"Good," I called after her as she disappeared.

For the record, this would come to be the first of hundreds of lies I would tell that dear lady. There was never anything good about watching her walk away.

But my many addictions were always steeped in a toxic brew of lies.

Would I ever find a path to full and complete honesty?

And if I am to use terms like *full* and *complete*, that honesty should probably not be restricted to just half the population of the planet . . . men.

Like American culture had begun to do with Billie Jean King, it was time for me to be inclusive of women, too.

I would eventually get and stay sober three years later, but I still somehow felt it was okay to trade one addiction for another . . . for decades to come.

It's a Date

"2-5-5-1-3-6-1-4-0-2-5-0," HARRY REPEATED.

I was lost. "And that represents . . . "

"The new numbers for January through December," he explained, then took a healthy pull on his beer.

My head was starting to hurt. Was it the dozen or so Kirins that Harry Nilsson and I had already consumed over lunch, or was it from me trying to understand this amazing trick he had just performed?

Give him a date, any date this year, and he could tell you what day of the week it was.

"So, no more 1 through 12 for the months," I replied, "now it's . . . 2-5-5-1 . . . say it again."

"3-6-1-4-0-2-5-0," he confirmed, "So let's do today, August 12, 1976 . . . you add 4, *the month*, to 12, *the day*, to 2, *the year*, and that gives you 18, which you divide by 7 . . . You don't care how many times it goes into it . . . you just want the remainder. Which is 4. The 4th day of the week. Thursday."

"I think I need another drink to fully digest that," I declared, and motioned the waiter over. We were enjoying a Japanese lunch at the Robata Room in Manhattan.

"You probably do," he reasoned. "Because 1976 is a leap year, so this

61

year is actually a 1 . . . up to and including the 29th of February. Then it becomes . . . " He motioned for me to finish.

"A 2?" I said, unsure.

"Bingo," he announced.

Harry and I both loved math, so I was doing my level best to keep up with him and learn this equation he had just shown me.

I was also trying to keep up with his drinking, which was a futile effort for all who dared. For the record, I only tried to outdrink the great Harry Nilsson once, about a year previous, and vowed I would never do *that* again.

That had been my first attempt to defeat a sitting champion. The second being Jack Nicholson's uncle and father figure, one Shorty George Smith, who I tried to unseat at the El Presidente Hotel in Durango, but John and Judy Belushi both rescued me from that deadly exercise, if you remember.

But, for our part on this hot day in Manhattan, Harry and I were both rather timid in our consumption. A dozen beers each over lunch was normally just a prelude to the proper intake of distilled spirits.

Harry had a business meeting to attend later that afternoon, so perhaps that was why he was basically on the wagon with just the twelve beers.

We finished our lunch, but as he left to go to his meeting, he turned and said, "Una and I are joining some friends for dinner . . . wanna come?"

"It's a date!" I said.

I always said yes to an evening with Harry and his wife Una . . . they knew the most interesting people.

They did not disappoint on this particular evening. For, after a short ride from the Navarro on Central Park South, we suddenly found ourselves in front of the Dakota.

I had already met a good many of Harry's friends . . . Eric Idle, John Cleese, and Graham Chapman. Harry and I were both *huge* Python fans. Another reason to love the man.

But I also knew who lived at the Dakota back then, and there was one particular couple that I knew to be friends of Harry's who resided in that amazing building.

Could it be? I wondered, as we rode up in the elevator. That question was answered quickly, as a moment after Harry rang the buzzer, John and Yoko were at the door.

Answering the door themselves.

After a few pleasantries, John looked me over and said, "I know you. How do I know you?"

As this was my very first real encounter with a Beatle, I was just trying to keep my face from crystallizing and shattering into pieces as it dropped to the floor. I managed to squeak out a timid "I was at the Troubadour one night when you were there, but I can't imagine . . . " (*Imagine!?* Shit. Did I really just say *imagine?*)

"Never mind that, come in," he said, as warm and inviting as anyone who has let me visit their home. Yoko was likewise warm and friendly.

There was no help in evidence, and we sat together and had a macrobiotic meal that Yoko had prepared, with me trying to treat this incredible artist the way he seemed to want to be treated . . . like just another bloke.

I somehow managed to do that convincingly, until: "Hold on!" he interrupted suddenly. "It's Steve, for fuck's sake . . . Louise Lasser . . . Yoko, help me." After which they both said in unison, "*Mary Hartman, Mary Hartman!*" As the evening shifted to any number of inquiries about the cast, the writers, Norman Lear.

All the while trying to just treat me like a normal bloke, as they gushed in their fandom of that quirky bit of seventies television.

It turns out there was another American television show that got the attention of John and Yoko one evening. The show was *Saturday Night Live*, and the episode came quick on the heels of a lot of speculation about a Beatles reunion.

All of it pure nonsense, as none of them were interested in that at the time.

But a good many promoters had made public what they would be willing to pay, should they ever change their minds. Each of these offers were for sums in the millions.

So, with that buzz as the backdrop, Lorne Michaels came onstage during the show a few months before and tried to place a competitive bid on national TV, in hopes of luring them onstage. Not for a full concert, just one or two songs.

He held an envelope in his hand, and in summing up he said, "I've spoken with the head of NBC, and we are willing to offer"—they zoom in as he holds up the check—"three thousand dollars!"

The bit had the desired effect, as the audience laughed loudly at this absurd lowball offer. What Lorne probably didn't know at the time was that John found it amusing, as well.

As did an old friend who was visiting from out of town. Paul McCartney.

John sat there and recounted this to Harry and Una and me, and claimed that he and Paul actually got in a cab and headed down to 30 Rock in hopes of walking away with $1,500, a fair price, they felt, as there were only two of them.

At some point on that journey, one (or both) of them changed their mind, and they never got to claim their reward.

Harry and Una and I left after another hour or so, and there were more pleasantries, all of which led to me leaving that night with their phone number. (What were they thinking?)

I thanked Harry and Una profusely for that incredible experience and said good night. But no sooner did I arrive back in L.A. but I get a call from my dear pal Buck Henry.

Buck and Lorne had learned of the John/Paul almost-show and wanted to give John a heads-up that they were going to sweeten the deal and increase the offer to $3,200, if even one of them chose to drop by. This was to happen during an episode when Buck was the host.

All those who know their *SNL* and Beatles history know that John and Paul never claimed their prize, but George did. But it gave me a legitimate excuse to call John and Yoko and tell them the plan, which they made clear would probably be another no-show. For my part, I just was elated to be the go-between between Buck and a Beatle.

And my friendship with Harry Nilsson just kept giving and giving.

I had quickly mastered his calendar trick and even taken it a bit further. What Harry had taught me was the calendar for the current year, which was at that time 1976. And, armed with that knowledge, it was not difficult to do the year before and the year after.

To curry favor with Harry, I started to memorize the calendars for a good many other years during the last century.

And when I say memorize the calendar, I mean I learned the number from 0 to 7 for the year in question, which I would add to the number of the month (that's the 2-5-5-1 bit), add that to the date you were trying to determine . . . okay, I know I've lost you.

But suffice to say, I started to commit to my fragile brain a good many 0s through 7s to make this equation work, and I could suddenly do people's birthdays, D-day, you name it.

I even went on *Letterman* in the eighties and did Harry's little calendar trick, but apparently, I did something wrong.

When Dave asked me what day of the week it was when *American Bandstand* premiered for the first time on August 5, 1957, I did the math and said, "That was a Monday" . . . to which Dave responded, "Ooh, I'm sorry . . . it was a Tuesday."

The audience gasped and laughed uncomfortably as I said, "Oh, shit!"

They bleeped that out, of course, but I did the calculation again, and came up with the same answer . . . Monday.

So my reputation had been stained. Till I finally figured out what I did wrong:

I believed Dave.

Or more accurately, his writers. I don't think they were deliberately trying to mess with me, but August 5, 1957, was definitely a Monday. Someone probably just made a simple typo.

But, back to '76: When I mastered most of the calendars of the previous century, Harry was duly impressed. So I was allowed deeper into the inner circle, which led to many days and nights shared with a certain drummer that we were both fond of . . . the beloved Ringo!

I was a drummer from age thirteen, but when Ringo came along . . . I just wanted to do *that*.

I got a Ludwig set like Ringo, I held my sticks like Ringo. I learned all the drum parts to all the songs he ever wrote or performed. I was never remotely as good as Ringo, or his brilliant son Zak, or the brilliant Jim Keltner, who I see every year at Ringo's birthday. Along with Ringo's beautiful wife Barbara, and her sister Marjorie (married to my dear friend Joe Walsh!). How lucky am I to know and still be close to friends like that.

How did this happen? How did I keep finding myself in such extraordinary company?

Friend of Harry and Una . . . come on in. Meet a Beatle.

Chat Cindy Williams up at a Christmas party, you get to meet Jack Nicholson.

I kept turning up with all these noted figures, and no one was really sure how I got there.

Least of all me.

A few years later Louise Lasser's ex-husband would make *Zelig*. About just such a character.

I could relate.

Cat Collar

WHEN SUE-SUE THREW A PARTY, it was sure to be a hooley.

Like me, Susan Tyrrell was not an artist who needed a weekend to let loose. She liked to keep an open mind and a well-balanced blood-alcohol level at all times, and that certainly included Monday through Friday, and by extension, the workplace.

But it was a warm dry weekend in L.A., and at this point she was living in an ideal party house in Hancock Park, and she had much reason to celebrate.

She had been nominated for a Best Supporting Actress Oscar for *Fat City*, starring Jeff Bridges and directed by John Huston.

My wife Ingrid and I had reason to celebrate as well, as we suddenly found ourselves invited to tonier gatherings like this one.

Perhaps because I had finally transitioned from my status as a Disney day player to more noticeable roles like Lester in Bob Rafelson's *Stay Hungry*, with Sally Field, Arnold Schwarzenegger, and the abovementioned Mr. Bridges.

Susan took to Ingrid right away, as they looked like they might be related; Ingrid was a far more angelic version of bad girl Susan Tyrrell, who earned that title honestly in Andy Warhol's *Bad*.

As the ladies got acquainted, I got my hands on a sorely needed drink and quickly found myself engaged in conversation with an erudite young man who was clearly a cinephile of the highest standing.

He knew all my father's films, and impossibly, he even knew a few of mine!

And, best of all, he was not stingy with that high-end blow that was turning us both into an even more scholarly pair.

At some point, it felt appropriate to ask this fellow's name, to which he responded, "Paul Schrader."

I tried to act nonchalant, but it was no easy task, as I am suddenly in the presence of the man who wrote *Taxi Driver*.

"You should know me. I'm putting you in my movie. Didn't Harold tell you?" he said between bumps.

I assumed he was talking about Harold Schneider, and he was, as Harold had produced *Stay Hungry*, and we had become quite close.

"First of all, shame on Harold. He did not. But more importantly, I'm a huge fan, so I'm prepared to do work in grip, electrical, or craft service in any project that you're involved in."

Apparently, I infused the right combination of flattery, cocaine, and alcohol into our first meeting, because Paul did cast me in his film.

And, as simple as that, I had just landed my biggest part to date, in a movie called *Blue Collar*, with big names: Richard Pryor, Harvey Keitel, and Yaphet Kotto.

Things were looking up.

A great script, written by an A-list writer, with A-list actors, and none of that Disney film morality to hold us back, onscreen or off.

In an unfortunate twist, Harold and Paul wound up in a major disagreement. To hear Harold tell it, everyone needed to just relax.

Blue Collar is a wonderfully dark film about the auto industry, Detroit, race relations, and much more.

After reading the first ten pages, the big three U.S. automakers at the time—Ford, Chrysler, and Chevy—sped away from this project as quick as their steel-belted radials could carry them.

But Harold was undeterred.

He was certain that we would have an ideal factory to film in at the Checker Motors plant in Kalamazoo, Michigan. All because he had heard a top executive's wife gush at the prospect of meeting some Hollywood celebrities if we were allowed to film at the plant.

Universal Pictures and Paul Schrader felt that was a bit precarious, and they let him go.

But on this particular matter, Harold turned out to be right.

Checker was happy to have us there. Never underestimate a woman's influence in any weighty matter. But Harold was gone by then. But not for long. We would still work on a film later that year, 1977, called *Goin' South*.

Back to the hugely talented Paul Schrader, who I must now heap an appropriate amount of praise upon, for what I can call a career.

Starting in the seventies and carrying on till 2002, my dear friend Paul has possibly gotten me more work than several of my agents.

In that time, I appeared in *Cat People*, *Blue Collar*, *Hardcore*, and *Auto Focus*.

All are jobs he just handed me. I didn't have to audition for one of them.

There are any number of good books available about this exciting time in film. *Easy Riders, Raging Bulls* by Peter Biskind is certainly one of them. It takes special note of the tectonic shift that occurred in our culture, and how slow the studio system was in keeping up with it.

But it was on this film, *Blue Collar*, that I became aware of a shift that had occurred in what kind of parts I was starting to receive.

I was starting to get the "Thomas Mitchell" roles.

For those under ninety, Thomas Mitchell is the actor who played Scarlett O'Hara's father in *Gone with the Wind*.

But when I say that I was getting his roles, I'm not speaking of playing the dad in the antebellum South.

I'm talking about drunks. He regularly played drunken Irishmen.

Can you take a wild guess as to why that was?

I believe it would fall under the heading of "continuity" in any and all production reports.

Why risk recording much footage of a sober Thomas Mitchell or a sober Ed Begley during principal photography of any given project? How are you going to use it?

How will it intercut with the vast majority of what you will be given . . . me in a fairly drunken state.

There are few standout moments that give a clear indication of why I hold this opinion.

We filmed in bars more than once during production, and the local beer was Stroh's, and for matching or continuity, I regularly had to summon the overworked prop man to fill my drink, as "my character" needed to have a large foamy glass of Stroh's before him in each and every shot.

All twenty-five of them. Just to keep things authentic.

There is a shot, in the actual movie, of me stumbling out to my car, barely able to stand, that required no prompting from our director. No "Action" or "Cut."

Just wild footage, grab it as you need it, me in my native habitat.

And my excesses were not confined to the set. Things occasionally got dangerous for me back at the hotel.

I remember being rip-roaring drunk but having a fairly normal conversation with Harvey Keitel on the mezzanine level of the Kalamazoo Hilton when I felt the need to spice things up a bit, so I started to climb over a guardrail, muttering something about how "I can't go on," and hung there, twenty-five feet above the lobby floor, for a very long twenty seconds, which elicited great shock, horror, and attention, which was exactly what I wanted, till I hoisted myself back up to the higher floor and safety at the last minute and casually took my seat at the bar.

Harvey has never looked at me the same since that day.

Hey. Worth it. Harvey Keitel noticed me.

Now, how would I get Richard Pryor to notice me?

This moment, likewise, held some risk, when we gathered to play a game of poker with a few of the actors one night.

It was Richard, Lane Smith, Harry Northup, Borah Silver, Paul Schrader, Cliff DeYoung, and me.

At some point during a lull in the action, I could not contain my worship and fandom of Richard any longer and said, "You know, your latest two albums changed so many lives, for the better, and mine was one of them."

To which he responded, "Yeah? What albums are those?"

Oops.

How do I answer his legitimate query without saying the N-word, not once, but twice? It's in both album titles.

"*Bicentennial Black Man*" and "*That Black Man's Crazy*" came out, without a beat, and then they sat there till Richard gave them his approval with a laugh, and all joined in.

He was nice to me before that, and even nicer after.

I knew that I hadn't the right to use that word, and he liked that I knew that.

A few years later, Paul gave me a lovely role in a remake of the noir classic *Cat People*, this time starring Nastassja Kinski, along with my dear old friend Annette O'Toole, and my new friends Malcolm MacDowell and John Heard.

We filmed half in Los Angeles at the Universal lot, and the other half in one of the most beautiful cities in the land, New Orleans.

Given the nature of my role, I had a fair amount of time off, so it was lunch at Commander's Palace and dinner at K-Paul.

I was newly sober at this juncture, and I remember so clearly the joy of being clear and present in how I approached every moment on that film, especially a rather grisly scene involving me and one of the big cats.

Spoiler alert for a half page.

As this was 1981, there was no CGI technology available for the effects, so when the big cat rips my arm off, it was done old-school.

I wore a fake arm, molded to look like mine, and in a series of shots to protect me from any real danger from the actual panther, we tore the fake arm right off my real body.

Red dye, Karo syrup, rubber bands to simulate tendons stretched and then broken, and damned if it didn't look pretty good.

But once the arm was torn off, it was my turn to get creative.

In any number of films, the reaction to that serious an injury is to scream bloody murder, because, well . . . your arm had just been ripped off.

But that seemed like the easy choice to me. More likely, I reasoned, was that the shock and trauma would be so great that my character, Joe, would more likely convulse on the floor as he bled out, looking to John and Annette with a look that clearly said, "I'm gonna be okay, right?"

Probably not.

And, since Paul is, and has always been, a great collaborator, he was 100 percent supportive of that choice, and it stayed in the final cut.

And this, and all of his films, are highly important works to this day.

One of his more recent films, *First Reformed*, which earned him yet another Oscar nomination for Best Original Screenplay, was about something as important as it gets: climate change, and how we accept it or deny it, at our own peril.

He has been an artist of tremendous vision for the past half century. Here's to many more years of inspiration for us all.

I'm Tapped

IT WAS AROUND 1974, AND Harry Gittes and Cindy Williams had decided to spilt up.

Sensing this was my moment, I made another tragic appeal for her affections, but Cindy had some fairly prudent house rules about dating a practicing alcoholic.

I decided to set my sights on a more realistic goal: keeping both Cindy and Harry as friends. I even offered to help with the move. Boxes were collected at the local market and brought back to Harry's. As the "his stuff"/"her stuff" was sorted, I was sure I'd be tossed in the "hers" box and forgotten by Harry.

He must have seen something in me that I had not spotted yet, as Harry and I remained good friends for another forty-five years.

And on the long list of impressive folks that he introduced me to, let's add one more.

After he and Cindy split up, Harry started to see this smart and beautiful woman, in every sense of the word, who went on to become an accomplished teacher and author, one Elissa Haden Guest.

There's a theory that talent can run in the family, and I think that might just be true.

Elissa's mother, Jean Guest, was a well-known casting director with a keen eye for talent.

She cast me in a series and a few other jobs, but please don't judge her by that.

Elissa's father, Peter, worked at the United Nations and he also had not one but three handsome and talented sons: Nick, Chris, and Anthony.

Though I know and love the entire Guest family, let me devote several pages to Christopher Guest and explain the profound impact he has had on my life and my career.

I first met Chris with Tony Hendra at a recording session for a *National Lampoon* project, and that certainly piqued my interest. The *National Lampoon's Radio Dinner* album had already been released, and it was a huge success. And for my money, Chris was the funniest thing in it.

Meeting him for the first time, I was shameless in tossing his sister's name around to gain favor, and we had a friendly but brief exchange. I was then reintroduced to him some time later when he moved to L.A., and we became friendly through my pal Bruno Kirby, along with my other friend Rob Reiner.

At one point, I even offered my meager skills as an assistant cameraman and assisted Peter Smokler on a film project that he and Chris were working on.

The talented Mr. Smokler went on to shoot *The Larry Sanders Show*, but before that, he filmed a unique little mockumentary called *This Is Spinal Tap*, which was directed by Rob Reiner and starred Chris, Michael McKean, and Harry Shearer.

At the time, Rob was married to Penny Marshall, who starred with Cindy Williams on *Laverne & Shirley*, a show that also starred Michael McKean and David L. Lander, and occasionally Harry Shearer, who started *The Credibility Gap*, with Michael McKean and David L. Lander, a brilliant radio show in the sixties and seventies.

There are really only two hundred people in L.A. The rest are extras that they bring in from Palmdale for the crowd scenes.

My career had just received a slight bump from being in *Mary Hartman, Mary Hartman*, and I was about to become slightly more famous for a fifteen-second appearance as John "Stumpy" Pepys in *This Is Spinal Tap*.

My scene was part of a look back at previous incarnations of the Spinal Tap band, and I was one of the many drummers who died under odd circumstances. My fate was to perish in a bizarre gardening accident.

The footage that we shot was to be part of a sizzle reel to secure financing for the project, but it proved to be good enough for the final version of the film, as its low-quality "kinescope" look only worked in our favor.

The film was a huge hit, and after directing *Spinal Tap*, Rob went on to direct *The Princess Bride*, *When Harry Met Sally*, and *A Few Good Men*.

For his part, Chris went on to direct and star in *Waiting for Guffman* with his good friend Eugene Levy, who co-wrote the script with him. They wisely also included Catherine O'Hara, Parker Posey, Fred Willard, and that whole wonderful troupe of actors who have made that film one of the favorites on many Top Ten lists.

And then, the unimaginable occurred.

I got a call from Chris and he explained that he was doing yet another film with many of the folks in *Guffman*, and would I like to play the assistant manager at the Mayflower Hotel.

I'd have scenes with Eugene and Catherine. Michael McKean and Michael Higgins. Parker Posey and Michael Hitchcock.

Steady now.

I have to back up for a moment and explain the state of my career at this particular juncture, December 1999.

I had appeared in many films as a supporting player but never really starred in any movies till the mid-to-late eighties, when I did *Transylvania 6-5000*, *Meet the Applegates*, and *She-Devil*. A savvy cinema buff will spot the common thread in those three films.

None of them were favorably reviewed, but more importantly, none of them did well at the box office.

There's plenty of wiggle room in the former. Not so much for the latter.

Since I was the common denominator in all three, and perhaps because I appear naked in at least two of them, they threw the book at me.

Yes, there is a three-strikes law in Hollywood, long before the statewide mandate of the same name.

So I found myself in movie jail for the entire decade of the nineties.

I will repeat . . . I did not get cast in any Hollywood movies for ten years . . . with two notable exceptions:

My friend Joel Schumacher gave me two weeks' work on *Batman Forever*, and Ron Howard and Brian Grazer gave me six weeks on *Greedy*.

To be fair, I could work on films . . . just not in this country.

I could go up to Canada and do a low-budget movie with a little girl and a bear. I could go to Australia and do a movie with a little girl and a kangaroo.

IMDb: *Ms. Bear* and *Joey*.

Enjoy.

And technically, I could even work on a movie stateside. It just had to be a certain category of film production. I hope you're still logged on to IMDb. Search *Santa with Muscles* starring Hulk Hogan.

I could certainly work in television, and I did, so I'm not asking you to throw a benefit. I just want to leave no doubt, I was in movie jail for a decade.

Until Chris sprung me.

He spoke on my behalf at the parole board (Castle Rock Entertainment) and made a case for early release . . . for me, and eventually for the film I had a small part in, *Best in Show*.

He made it clear that should I be paroled early, it was entirely possible that I would have gainful employment going forward.

He signed for my things and I promised that I'd never return to a life of cinematic crime.

And I was able to keep that promise, because Chris kept me off the streets with films like *A Mighty Wind*, which he wrote and starred in with Eugene Levy.

Then later, with the equally talented Mr. Jim Piddock on such films as *For Your Consideration*, *Mascots*, and the HBO series *Family Tree*.

To say I owe him is to understate.

Or, more accurately, owe them.

For it is not only Chris but also his amazing wife Jamie Lee Curtis who both help me keep my feet on the ground and my heart in my work as I try to duplicate what they have accomplished both in front of and behind the camera.

I try to practice gratitude on a daily basis.

Every day that I think of my friends Chris and Jamie, that gets all the easier.

Quidaciolu

I MET BRUNO THE SAME way I met any number of actors who were roughly my age . . . in an audition. We often found ourselves up for the same role, even though we were very different types.

He, an Italian American, who stood about five foot seven, with dark hair. I, a blond lad, about six-four.

But the hiring process for actors often casts a wide net. And by the time we sat in our third waiting room together, we struck up a conversation and soon learned we had much in common.

He was also the son of an actor, the immensely talented Bruce Kirby. And it turned out I had met his brother John Kirby years earlier, and even worked on a small film with him.

I was hitchhiking at this point, and as I mentioned in a previous chapter, that became more difficult post-Manson.

I instantly recognized that Bruno was one of the nicest guys I ever met, as he jumped at the chance to drive me back to the dreaded Valley, where he most certainly did not live.

He also introduced me to his wonderful and talented girlfriend, Annette O'Toole, and his amazing best friends, Tony Amatullo and Adam Arkin. Three incredible friendships that I maintain and cherish to this day.

This is now 1972, and at this point in Bruno's long career, his stage name was Bruce Kirby Jr. Like I said, we had much in common.

We did a Disney movie together called *Superdad*, and some other fairly light fare.

Then Bruno got even more serious about his work as an actor and decided to make some changes.

He started studying with Peggy Feury, and so did Adam and Annette, and so did I.

About this time, Bruno also decided to change his name. To the name he was born with. But not his full legal name, which is Bruno Quidaciolu Jr. He decided to split the difference and henceforth was known as Bruno Kirby.

He went on to give one brilliant performance after another in *Godfather II*, *City Slickers*, *When Harry Met Sally*, and *Donnie Brasco*.

I cannot begin to describe the influence this man had on me as an actor, but even more as a person.

I hope I've made it clear in previous chapters that I loved and respected my father, but he was not without his flaws (nor am I), as I think I've mentioned once or twice.

But in the thirty-four years that I had Bruno in my life, he taught me loyalty and kindness more than any friend or parent that came before or after.

It's not that my dad was devoid of those two important traits, but the greater emphasis was on Darwinism as the principal guiding force in most matters.

"Keep up, Eddie! You're gonna miss the train."

Which my dad was already on, and the doors were closing.

Or as I tried to keep up with my father in the driving rain:

"You'll remember your umbrella next time."

Let me be fair: I surely needed a lesson or three about remembering things, but in the rain and subway examples, I believe I was ten.

But this is not really about any neglect on my father's part. It is about a whole different way of thinking that was entirely foreign to me, but not Bruno.

We were both starving one day and went into a New York deli. Bruno got his sandwich first, so I said, "Dig in, Bruno. Mine's coming."

"I'm good," he said, and waited patiently.

"Bruno, seriously . . . I think I've thrown them with my vegan sandwich request. I know you're starving. If you don't dig in, I'm gonna grab your corned beef and run out of here . . . screw PETA!"

And he sits there forever till my tempeh BLT arrives.

Okay, that's not a good example. There are many who would do that when food comes in stages. How about this?

We're headed to the subway, and like that day with my dad, Bruno is the one with the actual appointment somewhere in Manhattan. I'm just along for the ride.

Unseen by Bruno, I stop for a moment to grab a paper and hand the guy some money, and Bruno is already down the stars to catch the Q train.

I race down the stairs as I hear the Q coming, insert my token (remember?), and as I race down the final stairs to the platform, I see the train pull away, and Bruno is gone.

Now what? I can't remember where we were going. No cell phones in '72. Will Bruno stop at a pay phone after his meeting? Leave a message on my L.A. answering machine that I can retrieve and meet up with him again?

I got my answer quickly as I spotted him hidden behind a column. Bruno had *not* boarded a train that he could have easily made. Now he would surely miss his appointment, for an actual paying job!

I was grateful but confused. "Damn. I'm sorry, Bruno. But why didn't you get on?"

"And leave you standing alone on a platform? That might be the way they do things in Hollywood, but here in New York, like the Marine Corps, we leave no man behind."

Okay, lemme stop. Maybe that's another bad example. You might have a loyal friend who would miss a train and an appointment so that you don't feel left behind.

But this loyal friend of yours . . . would they also:

Drive from Hollywood to Huntington Memorial Hospital in Pasadena to bring you healthy food and your mail as you lie there immobile . . . and do that daily . . . for six weeks.

Once out of the hospital, continue that pilgrimage to your home as you struggle in a full-body cast, and do that daily . . . for eight weeks. (More about that later.)

Help countless other good friends and new friends when he felt they were in need. Like Leopoldo Trieste, a wonderful Italian actor, who Bruno befriended on *Godfather II*.

Francis Coppola wound up needing Leopoldo for much longer than anyone expected, and he was stuck in a hotel, not knowing anyone, and not remotely fluent in English.

Bruno adopted this lovely man and regularly included him in his plans. He drove him everywhere he needed to go, took him on road trips, and really exposed him to American hospitality, which was still a thing back then.

And if Ingrid was my captain in helping me navigate through the choppy waters of early sobriety, Bruno was definitely my first mate.

We lost this brilliant and generous soul back in 2006, a few weeks after Ingrid passed.

I have not known another like Bruno, before or since.

But his memory is still alive among us:

Through his brilliant brother John, an incredible man and an immense talent, who I've known longer than I've known Bruno and is one of the most sought-after acting teachers in Los Angeles.

I know this, as I've been to his studio in Hollywood more than once, and seen his students soar . . . especially two of his students named Begley.

I also often see Bruno's lovely widow, Lynn Sellers, when she is in L.A. or I am in New Mexico. She is a brilliant actress in her own right who has been my dear friend for the past thirty years.

And I am regularly in touch with Adam Arkin and Tony Amatullo, two of Bruno's best friends, and mine. And double that with a young actor who Bruno welcomed to L.A. when he moved here from New York in 1978. Jeff Goldblum.

Trans 6

I'M NOT SURE WHY JEFF Goldblum is still speaking to me.

And that's not just my opinion. It's an opinion shared by others, including Dave Letterman, who after Jeff recounted being held up at gunpoint on my front lawn, did not mince words:

"You might want to steer clear of Ed Begley . . . there's nothing but trouble for you there. For all of us."

Jeff and the audience laughed, as did Dave. But was it a joke . . . really?

I've been dragging disaster to his door for over forty-five years.

Let me offer you tangible evidence that this is so.

In 1985, I was offered a starring role in a movie, and I was excited beyond words, as I had never been offered a lead in anything at that point.

It was a buddy movie, a comedy. And if I could just help them find a suitable funny co-star, they would close my deal, and we could begin shooting during my break from *St. Elsewhere*.

I think that Jonathan Axelrod, the head of New World Pictures at the time, might have even snapped his fingers when offering a novel casting suggestion: "Hey, how about your buddy Jeff Goldblum?" he put forth, like it was the first time it occurred to him.

It was all fairly subtle, but it was made known to me that if I could get Jeff to come on board, they would be able to finalize my contract. But absent that commitment from Jeff, well . . . there might be an opening available to me as a background artist.

Though this co-starring role in a buddy movie was a big leap in my career, it was not going to move the needle in Jeff's upward trajectory one iota. He had already starred in *Into the Night* with Michelle Pfeiffer, and *The Big Chill* with a stellar ensemble cast.

A case could be made that his career would not be helped *at all* by taking this role, but it might possibly do the exact opposite.

I nonetheless convinced Jeff that he should sign on to this epic, and by now, you might have figured out which epic I'm speaking of.

If you guessed *Transylvania 6-5000*, you would be correct.

For those who haven't had the pleasure of seeing this silly romp shot in Zagreb in 1985, you're in for a treat.

If you're ten or under.

But I should probably remind you that Jeff and I were both in our thirties at this point, and I was still laboring under the delusion that one can "fix the dialogue on set," or having already shot a scene, "fix it in post," as in postproduction, or editing.

I'm saying this as a man who has seen both things occur. But they are rare birds and don't always land on set, or in the editing bay.

We shot in and around Zagreb for seven weeks to complete principal photography, and nearly every day we violated Rule One of moviemaking:

What is Rule One?

Before you shoot any scene, you have a full and complete rehearsal, with all departments present.

That enables lighting, camera, sound, props, and everyone to see what is required of them. Then all departments go about their work, and when finished, the scene is recorded on celluloid or digitally.

We rarely did that.

What we did for many of our scenes was to rehearse the first page or two of the scene with all departments watching. Then our director, Rudy, would inevitably yell. "You get the idea. There's another page or two, but it's pretty much the same."

I found this unsettling the first time he did it, but assumed he knew what he was doing.

Jeff and I did as we were told, and cleared out of the crew's way so they could set lights and dolly track. We actors would finish in hair and makeup, and before you knew it, we would shoot.

But on the very first take, it became clear why I felt ill at ease earlier.

My last line was "Let's go check out the castle." And as Jeff and I headed in that direction, Rudy yelled, "Cut! What are you guys doing? You gotta exit this way," pointing to the right. "If you go that way," he said, pointing left, "the camera can't see you, so exit to the right."

I think Jeff spoke first. "Rudy, we have to go left. Remember the scene yesterday. We established that the castle is that way," he said, pointing. "We have to exit left."

This threw Rudy for a loop, but he soon realized it was true. "I think you're right. How do you like that?" His assistant director took charge and announced, "Give us a few minutes, folks. We're going to make a lighting adjustment, and we'll be ready for you in a bit."

And they relit the entire scene from the opposite direction, repositioned the camera, and relaid the dolly track.

We did this many, many times over the next seven weeks.

Somehow, Jeff was able to keep his cool. I wish I could say the same.

I finally flipped out one day, yelling, "It's hard enough to make one goddamn movie in seven weeks, but you're forcing this hardworking crew to do two! They have to set up every shot twice, because we keep violating Rule One! A full and complete rehearsal for all departments to see. Please, for God's sake . . . It's not fair!"

But circle the asshole in this picture, and it's not Rudy.

He just needed a tougher assistant director for his first movie. He just needed some more help, which I should have been better at dispensing.

You don't yell at someone on a set. You really don't.

That's Rule One.

The "full rehearsal for all to see" is Rule 1-A.

We actually had tremendous fun making this silly movie. I had met

Geena Davis years before with Dabney Coleman on *Buffalo Bill*, and I'm fairly certain that I introduced Jeff to Geena while we were watching dailies one night in Zagreb.

But I'm absolutely certain that Ingrid and I were the other two people in the room when they were wed in Las Vegas in 1986.

I worked with Geena on *The Accidental Tourist* in 1988, and she received the Oscar she so richly deserved for that fine work.

Circling back to the challenges before us in Yugoslavia.

I was feeling guilty about being so harsh with Rudy, and I made a pact with Jeff that no matter what happened from then on, we would be 100 percent helpful and supportive.

Given the day's schedule, this shouldn't have been hard, since the next scene was not complex.

Geena Davis, dressed as a vampire, enters through an open window as I lie sleeping. As she leans in to bite me, I wake up and start yelling, then Jeff comes in, but Geena is gone.

Classic Abbott and Costello "I just saw a ghost!" bit.

And my "helpful and supportive" vow gets even easier to pull off when we are told that the first shot in this simple sequence does not involve me in bed, or Jeff entering, or even Geena at the window.

It's simply a shot, quite necessary for editing, that features just the open window.

The Arri BL is set up with the proper lens. The lighting looks nice. Rudy had even asked our prop man, Repetsa, to hide just off camera and gently wave a small hand fan, so that the drapes seem to be moving ever so slightly in the breeze.

And the sound man can take a break . . . no audio!

Helpful and supportive just got real easy.

The camera rolls and Rudy calls out, "Comedy," which was starting to get annoying, as he said it in every scene instead of just saying "Action."

The camera rolls for a bit as Repetsa makes the drapes move ever so slightly, and . . . okay, it's been about thirty seconds . . . how much of this does Rudy think the editor needs?

But instead of "Cut," Rudy says, "Repetsa, gimme more fan. I don't see nuthin'!"

And the hidden prop man puts some wrist into it, and the drapes are *really* starting to move. I'm thinking, *Is there now a storm brewing in a rewrite we haven't seen?*

I raise my shoulders and mouth, "What the fuck?" Jeff pantomimes, "Zip it," so I shut up.

Rudy, undeterred, says: "Repetsa, I need to see some wind. Gimme some wind!" The poor prop man is now cramping up and starting to lose his balance, when I turn my attention from the window and spot Rudy, across the room . . .

Looking at the wrong window.

There are no lights or C-stands positioned around this other window. No Arriflex BL pointed at it. To this day, I don't know why he was looking out the wrong window.

But Jeff never lost his cool with any of that, or any of my hijinks when I was still drinking in the seventies.

Or any one of the many crazy stunts I pulled when we lived above Jeff and his first wife Patricia in an apartment in Hancock Park.

I would regularly accuse Jeff of stealing residual checks from my mailbox adjacent to his . . . which might have been funny the first three times I did it, but I don't know when to stop.

But Jeff never stopped helping me and Ingrid on a truly grand scale.

Jeff and Patricia watched our daughter Amanda for days when Ingrid and I were at Cedars welcoming our Nicholas into the world.

We shared fishing trips up at Lake Mamie in the Sierras. We played acey-deucey in the cabin at Wildyrie Lodge.

He was the first to introduce me to Trivial Pursuit, having played it with Len Cariou and then his castmates on *The Big Chill.*

He introduced me to Larry Kasdan, who gave me a great job in *The Accidental Tourist* starring Geena, Bill Hurt, and Kathleen Turner.

He bestowed on me the honor of being best man at several of his weddings, especially his magical current marriage to the beautiful and talented Emilie. A marriage that has blessed them with their two perfect sons, River and Charlie.

From the first moment I saw him in *El Grande de Coca Cola* at the Plaza Theatre in New York, I have been awestruck by the depth of his work as an actor and the range and versatility of the many characters that he completely . . . becomes.

If any of you out there are aspiring actors, go see anything that Jeff is in, and you will be likewise inspired. *The Fly, Jurassic Park*, and *Thor: Ragnarok* are a good start.

If you've seen him in *Seminar* on Broadway, you know why his theater classes have been among the most sought-after in Los Angeles.

Like Peggy Feury and Roy London, he has been a great teacher to me.

So, to the man who has made me a better actor since 1974, I say:

I've got a buddy movie I'd like you to read. It shoots in Antarctica.

Buckaroo Banzai

AS I SAID EARLIER, HARRY Gittes introduced me to many of the funny and talented artists that I have known, and topping that list in the writing category would be the brilliant writer and actor Buck Henry.

I had seen him on *That Was the Week That Was* with David Frost, and every person I have ever known loved his screenplay for *The Graduate*, and his performance in same. He played other great roles like Jack Dawn in *Gloria* with Gena Rowlands and wrote other great scripts like *To Die For* with Nicole Kidman.

I worked with Buck on *Protocol* with Goldie Hawn and became a close friend of his from 1972 till the time of his death a few scant years ago.

There is also another very strong connection with Buck.

About seven months after that disastrous evening that ended with a torn shirt, I found myself back at Tana's.

But this time I was not with Tom Waits but, instead, the charming Mr. Henry.

Buck had little interest in sitting or standing at the bar, so I secured us a nice table. But after we had finished our meal, we found ourselves missing the interaction that the bar afforded. So Buck proposed that I make a brief reconnaissance mission there and return to the table with some valuable intel.

Buck went so far as to point out one particular young lady who might want to spend some quality time with two available fellows, which we both were at that time.

Up to the bar I sauntered, sidling up to a spot just next to her, careful not to make eye contact, as I didn't want to spook her or, God forbid, give her the impression that Buck and I were there for anything but the gnocchi.

Before I could get out so much as a hello, this charming lady sized me up and said, "How are you doing tonight?"

I looked behind me to make certain that she was addressing me. She was. "Fantastic. How about you?" She just chuckled and added, "You don't remember me, do you?"

I have poor vision without my glasses, and I had ditched them earlier, hoping that it would make me more attractive. But up this close now, it became clear to me that we had indeed met.

"Hold on, do you live near the Sunset Marquis . . . you have a little dog?" I ventured.

"No, sweetie, I do not live near the Sunset Marquis, and I don't have a dog," she replied.

As I became more aware with each passing moment that I definitely knew this young lady, Mimi Machu clocks us having a friendly conversation, and announces, "Thank God! I'm sick of hearing about that goddamn torn shirt!"

And it all came back to me, and we all came back to Buck's table, and we all came back to Ingrid's afterward . . . oh wait . . . we didn't all come back to Ingrid's.

Just me and Ingrid.

We left Buck and Mimi at the restaurant. I'm not sure what they did for the remainder of their evening.

For my part, I fell in love with a charming, beautiful, and kind young lady who I would marry a whirlwind two months later and have two incredible children with, Nicholas and Amanda. And we wasted no time in getting started with Amanda. She was born less than a year after Ingrid and I were married in Vegas on Halloween of 1976.

Trick or treat, Ingrid.

It's important to remember how completely insane I still was at age twenty-seven.

I convinced Ingrid, my girlfriend of only two months, that the best way we could recognize All Souls Day in that bicentennial year was to hop in my Toyota Land Cruiser and head for Vegas to get all hitched up. The only way I can possibly explain this poor judgment on her part is to mention that I was sober at this point, having had the DTs for the first time at a motel in Marysville, California, a few months previous. I was there on a Jonathan Demme movie, *Citizens Band*, with Paul LeMat and Candy Clark. And Ingrid had seen me through my first bout with the DTs and had nursed me back to health in the process.

Get the Al-Anon ambulance for that dear lady.

Back to our wedding day. I remember vividly stopping in Barstow for fuel on Halloween night, with all the sons and daughters of the desert milling about in *Star Wars* costumes.

We had stopped at a Jack in the Box to get food and caffeine, but while in line at the drive-up, I was troubled by the rattling coming from underneath my car. A quick inspection made it clear that it was the muffler.

I found myself under my vehicle again, as I had been on the Sunset Strip the year before. But this time with a 10mm wrench, tightening the muffler strap, upon which the wrench slipped and clocked me pretty good on the nose.

There were no smartphones back then, and in our rush to Vegas we hadn't thought to bring a camera. And thank God. I am forever grateful there are no photographic records of this momentous occasion, as I looked like Jake LaMotta after his evening with Sugar Ray Robinson.

At the Clark County Clerk's office, I learned more about Ingrid, or should I say Margaret Darlene Taylor. She had been given the name of Ingrid by a Subud master, and I must confess she looked a lot more like an Ingrid than a Margaret Darlene.

I spared no expense for our wedding: the Candlelight Wedding Chapel.

I looked over at her several times, and I could tell she was having second thoughts, what with my bloody nose and face and all. But ignoring her better judgment, she croaked out an "I do" at the appropriate moment, and we were wed.

What happened next would have made any sane woman initiate the annulment process the same day.

I checked us into a low-end hotel, with a lower-end casino, and since our room would not be ready for another two hours, I mansplained what I thought would be best for us as a newly married couple:

I would play some craps till the room was ready and win back the price of the license and wedding.

Since they were offering free champagne at the craps table, I would start drinking again.

We would get her IUD taken out as soon as we got back to L.A. so we could start a family.

Only one of those things would work out well for us.

The starting-a-family part.

The choice to play craps looked promising at first. I did, in fact, win the entire cost of our wedding, license, gas, and drive-through dinner. But for a compulsive gambler, that win led to many much larger losses in the months to come.

Though the champagne was free, it would likewise prove to be a bad choice, for all the obvious reasons.

But eventually I found a solution for all that kind of bad behavior.

I would try to stop drinking with a group of people, rather than alone, and a short while later (three years), I would finally get sober and stay sober . . . to this day.

Yes, Ingrid and I would split up a dozen years later . . . but because I was no longer in my mad state, we would become friendly, then best friends, then like the closest of brothers and sisters, and we would remain so till she tragically passed in 2006 of a pulmonary embolism.

But if I ever miss her beautiful face, I need only invite my son out to lunch or dinner. And if I want to double my pleasure, he need only bring my granddaughter River along.

To my great relief, they both have the "Ingrid" look. Which is a good thing given that your other choice is the Ed Begley Sr. mug. A look that I'm taking on more and more every day.

You'll learn more about my wonderful children and grandchildren in the chapters ahead.

Indulge me, please. When you get there, don't flip through. They are remarkable people with great accomplishments, and they live green and simple lifestyles that rival mine.

That's what we want, isn't it? For our children and grandchildren to do as well as us, perhaps even leave us in the dust-to-dust.

To sum up this chapter, I'll only say . . . as horrible as it was to lose someone like Ingrid, someone that dear . . . I am forever grateful that I could make my peace with her.

And although Buck Henry passed away in 2020, I feel like he is still among us, too.

Lyndall Hobbs, Buck's old friend, brings us together often with Buck's wife, Irene Ramp.

And the gift of knowing them lives on.

Barely Skating By

HELENA KALLIANIOTES IS A GREEK actress and dancer who caught all of our attention after an impressive scene in *Five Easy Pieces* with her friend Jack Nicholson.

She was well-known before that for her formidable skills as a belly dancer.

I'm not sure when she moved into the back house at Jack's property, but she had been there a while when I first ventured up there in 1972. She lived there for decades and helped her friend Jack in many ways.

Being one of the most generous men I have ever know, Jack helped her (and me) in myriad ways, as well.

And the friendship I enjoyed with Helena took on another dimension when we worked on a film together in Birmingham, Alabama, in 1975.

It was *Stay Hungry*, a film I mentioned earlier, directed by Bob Rafelson, that also starred Jeff Bridges, Sally Field, and a new face on the scene, a bodybuilder named Arnold Schwarzenegger.

Helena and I became fast friends with Arnold on that film, but I must confess now what I thought of Arnold when we first met, which was: "Who is this meathead?"

At that time, I fancied myself fairly capable with my finances, so it seemed odd that I was having a problem with my landlord in Los Angeles, as my rent checks were bouncing while I was away on location.

I had a studio next door to my dear friend and artist Ed Ruscha, and getting the $75 rent to arrive in a timely manner was proving simply too difficult for me while I shot in Birmingham.

Arnold, the "meathead," was somehow not experiencing the same difficulty with his rent.

Probably because he didn't pay any rent, as he owned the building he lived in. Like he did the building where his offices sat.

I'm sure all of the readers know that Arnold is a Republican, and most are probably aware that I am not.

I am likewise certain that everyone will recall that Arnold served several terms as governor of California.

But he was one of those Republicans that I had to respect. He always protected a woman's right to choose, supported sensible gun laws, and was as serious about protecting the environment as any governor that came before.

You might have taken note of a recurring theme thus far on these pages. I have twice now heaped praise on gentlemen who sit on the other side of the aisle from me, but I do so quite deliberately.

I'm not stingy with my time and money in supporting progressive causes. But I also spend a lot of time trying to reach consensus, trying to find common ground with those with whom I might sometimes disagree.

But I'll tell a largely unknown story about Arnold, and you can tell me if he qualifies as a heartless Republican.

I was an avid fan of the *National Lampoon*, and soon became friends with Michael O'Donoghue, Tony Hendra, and Chris Guest during their time there, but this story involves Tony Hendra, during his tenure as editor.

Having heard of my friendship with Arnold, Tony had the temerity to ask me to contact him to do a photo shoot.

They were working on a "Gay Issue" of the *Lampoon*, and they wanted me to take a photograph of Arnold ironing a dress, with the title beneath to read "Iron Pumping."

I politely explained that I would do no such thing, as the very act of inquiring would be insulting to a manly man like Arnold.

Tony called me back repeatedly and asked what his response was, and each time I made it clear that I was not going to do it.

But this was the late seventies, and I still had (yet another) unfortunate character defect. I would repeatedly say no to something I didn't want to do, but if you asked me to do something, oh . . . around four times, I'd usually cave and agree to anything.

And Tony Hendra must have known this, as he quickly wore me down, and I called Arnold and gave him all the important details: him in shorts and a T-shirt, ironing a dress, "Iron Pumping."

What happened next was quite unexpected. Instead of a dial tone, I heard the sound of laughter on his end, and then: "This is funny. When do we do this, Eddie? You'll take the pictures, right?"

I mumbled through some dates, and one was chosen. I arrived at Arnold's, set up lights and a camera, and took the pictures. When I was done, I asked him how he wanted the check for the modeling fee made out. To which he remarked. "You keep that money, Eddie. You have a wife and kids; I don't."

It was instantly clear that he was doing it all for me. To help an out-of-work actor who had a young family. He went so far as to tell them to send me his fee.

There are probably many ways to think of Arnold Schwarzenegger. But I can't bring myself to regard him as the enemy.

But I started this chapter talking about his friend and mine, Helena Kallianiotes. And I'd be remiss if I didn't recount my next life chapter with her.

We were friends for years when Cher invited us both to her Monday night skating party in Reseda. And we went there every Monday for some time, until Cher had to go out on tour and Helena and I both found ourselves missing the skating.

Helena proposed that we join our collective phone lists and have our own skate night at the Sherman Square Roller Rink in Reseda.

We called it Skate-Away, and it became so successful that many believe that it helped create the roller disco craze that popped up a short time later.

That is, of course, pure speculation. But what is not remotely speculative is the episode of *Charlie's Angels* that I booked after some executives from Aaron Spelling's office came to our Skate-Away evening, scouting for talent on eight wheels.

I was offered a guest-starring role the next day.

Surely as a result of this well-crafted and edgy bit of TV drama, my acting career picked up, and I quickly ceded all control to Helena, as she was doing most of the work anyway.

As a founding member, I was given an embossed membership card as well as a jacket that bore my name. The skating night lasted for years and gave way to Helena's dance club downtown on Temple, of which I also became a founding member.

There was always a line at the door, and paparazzi at the door, as the food was always good, as was the music that prompted Helena to drag everyone out onto the dance floor.

Helena helped me in other ways before I got my big break on *St. Elsewhere*.

She once hired me to build her a pine table.

She might have really needed the table, but, like Arnold, I think it was more about helping out a friend during a tough time. And I was also game for any excuse to drive up to the property and visit with her and Jack.

And lest we forget: Just a few yards away sat the home of one Marlon Brando, an actor admired by me and everyone I knew at the time.

My reverence for Jack was deep, but I was always aware who lived just next door, and I longed for my lucky day when I'd catch Marlon walking down the driveway to get the paper or visit with Helena or Jack.

On the day that I was to deliver Helena's table, I nearly tripped over a burlap sack that sat on the doormat.

Once inside, I began to assemble the component pieces of the table in Helena's house, and Marlon's son, Christian, poked his head out of a room, looking worried as he asked, "Which door did you come in?"

"The front," I said.

"Be careful when you leave. There's a rattler in there," Christian cautioned. "I'm going to release it now that I'm done."

I waited for more.

"I brought it in when Dad was distracted with his ham radio. Freaked him and some guy listening in in Guam the hell out!"

The bar had been set high as to what was required to get a laugh out of Marlon.

As I finished setting up the pine table, Helena announced, "Did I tell you that Marlon wants to talk to you?"

My heart be still.

You Don't Know Jack

"DON'T BE SUCH A WIMP," said Ingrid. "Just pick up the phone and call him. You don't ask, you don't get" was her advice, as she continued converting our breakfast nook into a nursery. We lived in a one-bedroom apartment at Fairfax and Olympic, and our firstborn, Amanda, was due in a few months.

"You don't understand, everybody's always asking him for favors," I said. "I've never asked him for anything. To be honest, I think that's why he tolerates me."

It was true. Without me ever asking, Jack had been very generous with me over the years. He had invited me and Cass Elliot (from the Mamas and the Papas) to join him at the *Concert for Bangladesh* screening in Westwood. We had all piled into his Mercedes, smoked a joint, and walked the red carpet at the Bruin, then saw a wonderful film for a good cause.

I was still on the rotation for a seat beside him on the floor for Lakers games.

Why get greedy and ask for . . . a job?

And this would be a *big* job compared to what I was used to.

The film was *Goin' South*, and Jack was not only starring in it but directing. It was written by my friends Charles Shyer and Alan Mandel and produced by my other two pals Harry Gittes and Harold Schneider.

It seemed out of my league in 1977, but Ingrid kept pushing, and I finally caved and called Jack, knowing that'd be the end of my Lakers privileges, and more.

But that wasn't what happened. Instead, Jack said, "Let me talk to the boys, see what we can come up with. Gimme a couple days, Begs." And hung up.

It was only two days later when he called to tell me that he had found a role for me. "He's called Whitey, Begs. Should be a real stretch for you, playing a part named Whitey."

Ingrid was right: You don't ask, you don't get. I quickly learned that the cast would also include my friends John Belushi, Chris Lloyd, and Danny DeVito, as well as a very charismatic new actress that Jack had discovered: Mary Steenburgen.

Though I worked on that film for several months, I had lots of time off, so I could install myself in the lobby bar at the El Presidente Hotel in Durango, Mexico, and bond with a couple of great guys: Mr. Jim Harrison and Shorty George Smith.

Jim was a talented poet and novelist who went on to write *Legends of the Fall* and any number of novellas. He also had a healthy thirst, as I remember.

Shorty was a railroad man and was Jack's brother-in-law, who turned out to be Jack's uncle, married to Jack's sister Lorraine, who turned out to be his aunt.

(I apologize for not supplying a flowchart to illustrate who Jack and I thought our family members were and who they, in fact, actually were.)

Shorty was also the undefeated champion in all forms of competitive vodka consumption and dispatched me quite handily in a morning and afternoon session that ultimately led to John and Judy Belushi becoming actively concerned for my well-being. So much so that they dragged me out into the air and sunshine.

But that bit of overreach on my part was short-lived, or should I say Shorty-lived, as my "hold days" had come to an end, and it was time to get to work on camera with Jack Nicholson and that impressive cast.

In the scene, I tell Henry (Jack) that the bank is closed, to which he responds by pulling a gun on me as he *withdraws* all of Julia's (Mary Steenburgen's) gold from the vault. Then I am to say, "I would've never figured you doin' this to Julia" as I help carry the loot out to Henry's waiting wagon.

Jack was looking a bit concerned during the rehearsal but found a few choice words that enabled me to marginally improve. But after all the wider coverage, and even one attempt at my close-up, he could see that it wasn't really getting much better and said, "Is that all you're gonna give me, Begs?"

My first reaction was pure panic. I was both acting with and being directed by an artist that I admired like no other, and who I wanted to please like no other.

Then I remembered that Christmas car wreck on Sunset a few years earlier, and I decided to once again make terror my friend. I stepped away from the camera, faced a wall, and kept repeating, "I'm not feeling panic. I'm feeling energy."

When I returned and tried another take, the adrenaline that Jack had unleashed made it look like *something* was going on behind my vacant eyes. and I got a thumbs-up from him.

He seemed happy, so I was happy, and we moved on to another scene. But his words haunted me for some time . . . "Is that all you're gonna give me, Begs?" And it became obvious that he was absolutely correct.

As an actor, I was still stuck at that very low level of skill that I had achieved in 1969 on *Room 222*.

I was relaxed. Or, if something set me off, I was panic-stricken. And that wasn't good enough for Jack. And I instantly realized . . . it wasn't good enough for me either.

I got the part of Whitey by calling up a friend and asking for a favor. Not because I gave the best reading during the audition process. My white privilege now had to be expanded to include "Whitey" privilege.

Earlier that year (1977), I had been also handed the part of Bobby Joe in *Blue Collar*.

No audition . . . my friend Paul Schrader just gave me the part. As he did with *Cat People*, *Hardcore*, and *Auto Focus*. I was getting these parts, but . . . did I deserve them?

To answer that question, I needed to go back to class and begin to learn and grow again as an actor. So, like my friend Bruno Kirby, that's exactly what I did.

Most actors would agree that you can work with many different teachers, and then . . . one day someone says something that clicks, and you jump ahead, leapfrogging over several barriers, and find yourself in touch with a greater range of choices as an actor.

Such was that moment when Jack said, "Is that all you're gonna give me, Begs?"

And when I was ready to dig deeper still, a man named Roy London magically appeared. I had only worked with Roy a few days when he let loose with this little gem:

"You know what I think is the most interesting thing to watch? How a character deals with pain. Comedy or drama, it doesn't matter, but that struggle with physical or emotional pain is always the most compelling thing to watch."

I nodded politely and pretended to agree, but I can promise you I did *not* think that was a true statement, at all.

I said goodbye to Roy and started to drive home, thinking: "Oh, brother . . . really? That's what you want to watch? People writhing in pain all the time? Jesus, Roy."

But when I hit my first red light and had a moment to really think about it, I realized that that was not what Roy had said.

He said nothing about a character writhing in pain, or even demonstrably *being* in pain.

What he felt compelling to watch was "how a character *deals* with pain."

I instantly realized that was true for me, as well.

How, from the beginning of *Sophie's Choice*, you know that Sophie is struggling with something big, and over the course of the film we learn what that pain is, and we (like Sophie) are never the same.

Meryl and Viola Davis both in *Doubt*. Hell, Viola in anything, Meryl in anything. Joaquin Phoenix in *The Master*. Joaquin in anything.

And comedy! How a character deals with pain is still the most compelling thing to watch.

Laurel and Hardy are carrying a piano down a flight of stairs, and they fall . . . carrying a piano! Harold Lloyd, hanging from a clock.

Cheri Oteri at the pharmacy counter. Dabney Coleman in *Buffalo Bill* or *9 to 5*.

Do I need to mention my dear friend Don Rickles? Painful, hateful, dangerous things said to friends and strangers in the audience, sometimes to me. But I've never witnessed bigger laughs, for five decades.

That discovery, courtesy of Roy, was my biggest leap forward as an actor since I watched Jack in those Corman movies and thought I wanted to do *that*.

And I'm well aware that I can never do the *that* that is his spectacular career, but I can get better at it. And, with his help, I did.

The fact that he remembers my birthday every year, has allowed me into his home countless times, let me sit beside him at Lakers games, and even allowed me to become close to his three wonderful children, Jennifer, Lorraine, and Ray, only demonstrates how thoughtful and generous a man he is.

But his honest question, that truth that he somehow infused with absolute kindness, is perhaps one of the greatest gifts he has ever given me.

A lesser friend would've thought, *You can't handle the truth*.

Sorry. I couldn't help myself. It was right there.

If the Plug Don't Fit

IT'S MARCH 1979, AND I had just gotten a plum part on a TV movie with Tim Bottoms and Rip Torn called *A Shining Season*. I had been on *Mary Hartman* a few years earlier but was now starting to get better parts, as I had been in *Goin' South* with Jack, *The In-Laws* with Peter Falk and Alan Arkin, and *Blue Collar* with Richard Pryor, Yaphet Kotto, and Harvey Keitel.

My wife Ingrid was with me, and since ABC was paying, we were seated in first class as we headed to Albuquerque. Suddenly, Ingrid nudges me and subtly directs my attention to a couple seated behind us, but all I see is a rather handsome fellow with eye shades on and an attractive blond lady reading a magazine as he slept. I shrugged and mouthed, "What?"

Ingrid mouthed back "O. J. & Nicole." And a subtle look behind me made it clear she was absolutely right.

Then, and now, I'm not a guy who's going to bother someone on a flight, but after some time, he stood to get something from the overhead and smiled at me and Ingrid (maybe it was just Ingrid). We chatted with them both for a bit, and he even autographed a playing card for Ingrid. They returned their attentions to each other, as did Ingrid and I, and we said our goodbyes after landing.

He was doing a film project in New Mexico, and the next day we spotted them at the pool, as we were all staying at the Hilton in Albuquerque. We saw them repeatedly at the hotel and they were both quite charming.

Years went by, and I had heard that they had split up but never knew why. Then in 1989, a full decade after the Hilton in Albuquerque, I myself am likewise divorced and I spot O. J. at the China Club in Manhattan.

We probably sat there for two or three hours, commiserating and trying to figure where we went wrong in our marriages. I conceded that I had made one or two mistakes, to which he responded, "I really messed up with Nicole."

To which I responded, "Hey . . . buddy . . . so did I with Ingrid."

To which he then responded, "No, I *really* messed up with Nicole."

Had he not heard me the first time? "Hey, we all make mistakes."

All he said was "Yeah!", but in a manner that conveyed "You don't know the half of it."

If ignorance is any defense, I will plead it. As I had no idea of the spousal abuse that was occurring during and after their divorce.

I did some hurtful things to Ingrid, but hitting was not on the list.

At one point, Nicole started to document her injuries with Polaroids stored in her safe-deposit box.

A year later, and still woefully unaware of the abuse in their relationship, I spent time with O. J. in Ixtapa Zihuatanejo, Mexico, for a Marjoe Gortner Celebrity Sports Invitational.

And, when we got back to L.A., I would often be invited to his house for parties. But this was 1992, and the range of my electric car was quite limited, so I often needed to get a charge. He couldn't have been more helpful.

"Just pull right up to the garage. There's a plug on the wall. Kato will show you."

Yes, that wall. That Kato.

I watched the trial. I was in the courtroom for closing arguments. Nearly all those convicted of murder are in prison as a result of *one* piece of physical evidence. *One* piece of hair. *One* strand of fiber. *One* drop of blood. In this trial there were thirty-eight pieces of credible physical evidence. Much of it hair and fiber and blood.

I know some feel otherwise, but I do not believe that O. J. was ever going to be convicted (or get off) because of race. This was a trial about money. And the rich guy got away with it.

And I'm fairly certain that the rich guy has gotten away with it before, and since.

I became friendly with Robert Blake starting in 1975, when I did an episode of *Baretta*.

I played a dog handler (like I did in *Columbo!*), and then we reconnected at an environmental march and rally, and we started to spend time together, and he even became a regular at my Saturday pancake breakfasts at my home.

I respect the decision of the courts that have found him not guilty, but I will just share a couple of things that actually happened, as sure as the not-guilty verdict.

My first wife, Ingrid, and I were having some serious trouble, but she immersed herself in fixing up our new place in Studio City. She had found a very nice French fellow named Pierre who was painting our house, and that project seemed to go on and on. Till it soon became clear that Pierre was spackling more than the drywall.

Ingrid had gone to New York to see *Phantom* with him, bought some clothing for him at a Times Square men's shop and even a fairly nice keyboard and other audio equipment.

I suppose I was bellyaching about it a bit to Robert, but his reaction was quite different than mine. His neck and shoulders seemed to change shape as he asked, "What are you going to do about that?"

"What can I do?" I responded, sitting on fairly strong legal ground, given the nature of California community property statutes, and of course the karmic laws at work to balance out my horrible behavior over the years.

He looked me like I had three heads and reminded me, "You remember that I'm Italian, right?"

"Of course," I responded, though not really sure how that was germane.

"'Cause that's not the way we do things in Italy, or Little Italy."

I answered, "I'm not really sure what you mean," when I was probably quite sure what he meant.

He went on, "Someone takes my money, gives it to the house painter, and they're sittin' on planes and at Broadway shows . . . I'm gonna make a call and there's gonna be a last-minute rewrite on this little episode, and dat's da name a' dat tune."

I found it a bit unsettling but figured it was just tough talk from a guy born in a different era.

Then that horrible event occurred up at our mutual friend Marlon Brando's house involving Marlon's son Christian and a Tahitian gentleman named Dag Drollet. Dag had been seeing Christian's sister for some time, and Christian claimed that he had slapped Cheyenne around, and that his gun had gone off in a struggle.

Sometime after that horrible chain of events, I got a call from Robert, asking if I was still in touch with Marlon. I replied that I was, to which Robert responded, "It's too late now, but I always told him to call me when he's in trouble. I know things you can do." Curious, I asked, "Like what?"

"You rub your hands in pasta sauce, and they can't prove you fired a weapon. You find a dumpster"—yes, he said that—"and there goes the gun."

I heard that I was on a list to testify at his trial, but I was never called. The one assertion he made that was hard to swallow was that he "dropped his gun at the table at Vitello's, then later went back for it."

The flooring at Vitello's was not carpeted then, or now, so the notion of him dropping his weapon and not hearing it is hard to believe.

More importantly . . . in the many times he came over for pancakes, he never once removed his jacket, no matter how ungodly hot I would let it get in the summer.

And I always understood why.

If he had removed his jacket, all would have seen what I knew to be there underneath, whenever he left home. His sidearm never left his side.

I finally came to recognize that my relationships with O. J. and Robert had both sprung from my addictions and my infidelities.

I smoked a joint with Charles Manson. I regularly put myself and others in great danger in my drug and drinking years.

Was I also addicted to danger, now that I was in recovery on some other destructive behaviors? The only way to find out was to stop all my bad behavior. But was I ready?

Soon.

In the meantime, there was important work to be done for folks with far fewer resources than me and Robert and O. J.

The folks who help put food on our table every day.

Cesar & Ruben

I NEVER MET MAHATMA GANDHI, Dr. King, or Mother Teresa. But I knew Cesar Chavez, and he was the closest thing to a saint that I ever encountered in my long life.

There are a few other contenders for Hero's Hall of Fame status, like my dear friends Dolores Huerta and Vandana Shiva, but let me focus now on my lifetime hero and a man that I know inspired those two powerful ladies . . . and me.

Cesario Estrada Chavez.

Like so many of my friends at Valley College in Van Nuys, I stopped eating grapes when I heard of the injustice in the fields back in the sixties.

Not only were the wages shockingly low for backbreaking work in the sweltering heat, but there were few (if any) bathroom breaks, and very often . . . no toilets.

These uncomfortable facts were made known to me by my two dear friends from Valley College, Jan Fischer and Bill Molloy, who were way ahead of me on social justice issues, or whatever we called it back then.

No uvas! I'm with you . . . no more grapes.

No lechuga . . . no more lettuce. (I cheated a little and grew my own.)

I wanted to do more, so I heard about the union that Cesar and Dolores had started, United Farm Workers, and I started sending money in support.

This is all a bit of background to give context to a chance encounter at Pann's Restaurant in Inglewood in 1986.

I stopped there for breakfast on my way to LAX, and just as I was tackling my steel-cut oats, I see a car pull up that has a good many miles on it—a modest car at best—and two gentlemen get out, and one of them sure looks like Cesar Chavez.

But this is 1986, and Cesar has long been established as an internationally known labor leader, so I couldn't imagine he would be traveling in this modest car, but I instantly realized . . . that was *exactly* the kind of car Cesar would be traveling in.

This was not Jimmy Hoffa or Walter Reuther. This was a man who lived an unglamorous life like the farmworkers he represented. He and his wife Helen had both worked in the fields for years.

But as the two gentlemen entered and took their seats at a table, there was no doubt that this was that same great man that I had been supporting from afar since 1967.

After waiting for an appropriate opening between ordering and receiving their food, I approached respectfully and introduced myself, and met Cesar and his friend Irv.

"Mr. Chavez, Ed Begley. I'm a big supporter since 1967. If there's anything I can do to help, please let me know." And I handed him my card, which read:

Ed Begley Jr.
"Since 1949"

. . . as it does today.

He found that quite amusing, and asked what my passion was, and I told him that I had been an active environmentalist since the first Earth Day in 1970.

"Important work," he said. But then he waited to see if I had more to say on the matter.

I did. "But I try to remember that it's not just the owls and the whales that need our help, it's the people." When I continued, in some detail, to talk about the sick kids, and the cancer clusters in McFarland and Earlimart, he really started to warm up to me.

He took my card and promised to call, and of course he did. And then Irv did, then Jocelyn Sherman did, and Judy Martinez did, and then Artie Rodriguez did, and I soon found myself a part of the extended Chavez family.

A family that marched together, stuffed envelopes together, and did construction work together at the UFW headquarters in Keene, California.

In the many years that I knew Cesar and supported the cause, I am beyond grateful for his many victories. He fought for (and got!) drinking water in the fields. And lavatories.

He secured a health plan for the farmworkers and named it after his dear friend Bobby Kennedy. And likewise started a pension plan named after our fallen brother Juan De La Cruz, killed on the picket line.

But even with his many successes, he knew we had to be vigilant, lest the modest gains we had secured be weakened or taken away all together.

Which is happening as I write these words. Farmworkers are still dying in the heat in California.

I remember attending an environmental film festival in Colorado Springs in 1991 and walking to a nearby Catholic church, lighting some candles, and praying at his side for the children sick and dying in the cancer clusters of the Central Valley.

Cancer clusters that Cesar and I both believed were a result of misuse and overuse of pesticides, herbicides, and fungicides in those agricultural communities.

I saw him a short time before his death at a big environmental event up in the hills of Malibu, overlooking the ocean.

And then one day in 1993, I had both the extreme sadness and incredible honor of carrying his coffin through the streets of Delano.

I've been to a good many funerals in my seventy-three years, but I have never seen anything like this. Thirty-five thousand mourners had shown up to pay their respects to this great man.

On the tenth anniversary of his death, I had the additional honor of mounting a show about his life's work called *Cesar and Ruben*, which I produced with Jarlath Dorney and Stephen Roseberry. It won a Nos Otros Award and four Valley Theater League Awards.

In 2004, his family presented me with the Cesar E. Chavez Legacy Award for my years of advocacy for the cause.

I also have the extreme honor of knowing the great activist Dolores Huerta, co-founder of the United Farm Workers union, and I continue to work with her to this day on a number of social justice issues.

She has come to see my humble play about Cesar Chavez and Ruben Salazar multiple times, and has always seemed to enjoy seeing the various changes I have made over the years.

She has regularly helped me to make it more relevant to the challenges that the farmworkers have today, and to ensure a more thorough and accurate telling of the story of what has come before.

Make no mistake . . . she has paid a steep price for her commitment to social justice over the years.

She was clubbed and beaten badly and still faces many health challenges as a result of those injuries. She received the Presidential Medal of Freedom from President Barack Obama, an honor she richly deserves.

I'm often asked why I'm so committed to the cause of the farmworkers, Cesar, and Dolores. I'm certainly drawn to it because it's a just cause that can use a lot of help.

But it's also a function of where you are born, and when you are born.

In my case, the answer is Los Angeles, California, and September 16. Mexican Independence Day.

Can we continue to advance the cause of protecting the folks who help put food on our table every day?

Si, se puede!

Let's Move Elsewhere

"SCREW IT THEN, LET'S MOVE. Let's list the goddamn house and move, cause I can't do this anymore," I offered as a way out of our dilemma. My wife Ingrid was silent at first, because she knew that something, indeed, had to change.

We had been going over our mountain of credit card debt, and our first, second, and third trust deed mortgages, trying to see a way out.

We had bought the house two years earlier, when work was steady, but now it was 1982, and I was experiencing another lull in my acting (career?) that made it difficult each and every month to just pay the minimum on our many lines of credit.

Since this was our first home, we foolishly got a variable-interest-rate loan. It was an onerous loan that started at eleven percent, and was now headed well north of twelve percent, and climbing.

I was always handy, and I had recently gone to L.A. Community Adult School and taken a woodworking class, so with those more advanced skills, I could generate extra income doing handyman work for my friends who had money and a real career.

I did construction work with my pals Steve Steinman and Tom Long for the architect Frank Gehry.

I built a shed for David and Kathy Lander, a wooden fence for Michael and Susan McKean, and of course, the infamous pine table for Helena that would pique the interest of her neighbor, Marlon Brando.

I had set up a nice little shop in my garage and made wooden trays and racks that were sold on consignment at a shop on Larchmont Boulevard, just two blocks from our home in Hancock Park. A home that I was now proposing that we sell.

Ingrid, ever the cooler head, tried to bring down the temperature.

"Okay. So we move . . . to where? Back to an apartment? Have you seen what rents are like now? And no yard for the kids to play?"

"No, no, no," I said. "We'll still live in a house . . . just in a cheaper market. Hancock Park was an overreach."

Ingrid was growing concerned that I was serious about this. "So, we move," she repeated. "Where did you have in mind?"

"Atlanta," I blurted out. "We sell this place, and take that cash and get a nice house in Atlanta."

"You're serious?" she said. "And what will you do for work?"

I feigned outrage at the very notion.

"I've been to Atlanta many times! I've done films there, worked clubs there. I opened for David Bromberg at the Great Southeast Music Hall. I did a movie there with Harry Dean! I'll be a big fish in a small pond. Get a job at the local TV station . . . "

"Doing what?" she further inquired.

"Local weatherman. Local talk show! I know all the musicians and actors that come through town there. The local network affiliates will get in a bidding war over who's gonna get me," I boasted, knowing that probably wasn't true, but I was saved the embarrassment of hearing Ingrid say it by the ringing phone.

"I'm serious about this," I said as I answered the phone. "Hello."

Ingrid waited patiently as I listened to the caller on the other end. It was a man named Eric Klass, and he was using words that I didn't understand. "Slow down, what is a Saint Elsewhere? What does that even mean?"

I listened as Eric explained that it was a new medical show from

Bruce Paltrow, who had done *White Shadow*. And this was not just a pilot but a full thirteen-episode order by NBC.

"When do they want to see me? And when can I see a script?"

Since Eric was my agent at the time, he was able to answer those and all other questions. I headed over to the MTM lot in Studio City to pick up a few pages of a script that I would quickly learn and read for that same day. The part was Dr. Peter White, and he was a regular on the show, and I'll tell you right now I was sure that I nailed it. Until Eric called me and told me:

"You didn't get it."

My first thought was *That reading felt really good today. What the hell did I do wrong?* But, sober three years at this point, I had begun to look for something positive to take away from any perceived defeat. "What were they looking for that I didn't bring to the reading?" I finally asked.

"Nothing! They just wanted a different type," said Eric.

"Different type, huh? Who'd they get?"

"Terence Knox," said Eric.

In a situation like this, you're kind of hoping that you lose a part like that to a bigger (or equivalent) name. "Ed, you lost out to Jeff Goldblum." I'd think, "I would've been good in this part, but Jeff? Jeff is going to be even better." No attempt at false modesty . . . it's just true.

You get to a place where that sort of thing happens with your friends from time to time, and it doesn't really sting, because it feels like it's all in the family.

I was once in a room with the following actors: Paul Winfield, Paul Dooley, Max Wright, and Charles Kimbrough . . . and yes, we were all there for the same part!

I was slightly giddy before and after I read, and not the least bit upset when I didn't get it, because I thought, *I'm on the same list as Paul Winfield?*

I've lost parts to Steve Martin, John Cleese, Martin Short, and Chuck Grodin. And my reaction was the same each time: *I'm on a list with them?*

But when I heard I didn't get this part on *St. Elsewhere*, and it was to be played by a gentleman named Terence Knox, I was not as supportive, but only because I had never heard of him.

Jump ahead a few scant weeks when I would meet the talented Terence Knox, and it soon became clear how he got the role of Peter White over me. He was a fine actor who had already done *Used Cars* and *Heart Like a Wheel*. And he had a very different look than me, so it all began to make sense.

We ultimately became friends and even shared a dressing room, but none of that was known to me at the time (no IMDb then), so Ingrid was even beginning to buckle after I made a new case for my proposed radical change:

"Ingrid, sit down."

She did.

"I've been an actor for fifteen years. I don't care if you've chosen a career in sales, entertainment, or medicine. If you can't see some measurable results after fifteen years, a decade and a half . . . Hey, I'm not saying I want to quit show business. Just shake it up in a new market. Try something else."

Then my phone rings again. This time Eric tells me that they liked me so much that they want to offer me *another* part, Dr. Victor Ehrlich. Steady, lad.

Eric says, "Calm down. You'll only be in one, maybe two episodes, and you only have two lines in the pilot, but they're thinking of merging it with another character, Stanton."

"Who's Stanton?"

Eric says, "He wasn't in the draft you read. It could be tricky because one of Ehrlich's lines is *to* Stanton, so if they do that, you'll be talking to yourself." But he adds, "You never know, if the writers see something they could write for, there could be more episodes down the line."

I was given a time and day for my wardrobe fitting, and I promised Ingrid I wouldn't list our home for sale just yet. Perhaps something might come of this small two-line part.

I drove to the MTM studios and met Bob Moore, the wardrobe

Ed Sr. and wife Amanda Begley on shipboard, 1947

Ed Begley Sr., 1951

Allene Sanders, a magician's assistant and page at NBC. Would soon bear two children for Ed Sr.

Sister Killean's class at Curé of Ars, 1961

Boy Scout Ed, 1961

Eds Jr. and Sr., and sister Allene, 1962

Cindy Williams at Idyllwild, California, 1972

Ed's Studio City Bungalow in 1974 (disposal of human remains not included in rental agreement)

Harry Gittes and his dear mom, 1974

Longtime friend Neil Rhodes, 1974

Arnold Schwarzenegger, Birmingham, Alabama, 1975

Ed onstage at the Troubadour, 1975

Michelle Phillips, 1975

Groucho Marx at home, 1976

Mary Kay Place, 1976

Judy and John Belushi, Hal Trussell, and Ed—*Goin' South*, 1977

Author Jim Harrison—Durango,
Mexico, 1977

Tom Waits with Ed and Ingrid Begley, 1977

Louise Lasser—*Mary Hartman,
Mary Hartman*, 1977

Harry Gittes and Jack Nicholson—Durango, Mexico, 1977

Ingrid Begley, Bruno Kirby, Annette O'Toole, and Tony Amatullo, 1977

Set of *Blue Collar*, 1977. Paul Schrader directs Richard Pryor

Alan Arkin and Peter Falk on the set of *The In-Laws*, 1978

Eve Babitz, 1979

Christopher Guest, 1981

Jeanette Pierre, 1984

Ed and Jack at a Lakers game, 1989
(Credit: Rick Stewart/Allsport)

Ed and Annette Bening, 1991

Ed laying his dear Cesar Chavez to rest, 1993 (Photo by Jocelyn Sherman)

Ed in the Klamath-Siskiyou
Forest in 2002

Ed cooks a vegan meal for Oscar nominees in 2013: Hugh Jackman, Bob De Niro, Alan Arkin, Tommy Lee Jones, Joaquin Phoenix, and Daniel Day-Lewis

Ed and Rachelle Carson, 2022
(Photo by Russell Baer)

designer. And he had a few different lab coats for me to try on, along with some fairly nondescript stuff to go under it. But he also had two or three Hawaiian shirts laid out.

I asked, "Who are those for?" and he said, "You. I asked one of the writers where Ehrlich was from, and he said California, so I thought this might be fun."

"Huh . . . California? I did not know that."

I certainly knew that the series took place in Boston, but I was happy to learn this additional news about where my character was from.

Wardrobe fittings are always very important events for an actor, essential in the development of the character.

But they are often very important for another reason. I have many, many times learned at the wardrobe fitting: "They've changed the schedule. They're shooting your six-page monologue tomorrow now."

Or, "The junkyard in the Valley didn't have the right look. They're gonna shoot it in Barstow."

Or, "Your character is from California, and he's fond of Hawaiian shirts."

And even though I want to remain true to *my* vision of who my character is, I must also adapt to changes coming from the writer and the director.

And I would also extend that consideration to department heads, like Bob. If he thinks a Hawaiian shirt is a good idea for Dr. Ehrlich, let's give it a fair hearing.

And it received just that.

Bob and I walked over to the producer's office to show them Ehrlich's "look." John Masius and Mark Tinker seemed to like it. Josh Brand and John Falsey were on the fence, and then Bruce Paltrow joined the group.

He stopped in his tracks when he saw me: "What is this?" was his opener. He didn't seem pleased.

Bruce was not in the room when I read for Peter White, the part I didn't get, so this was our first encounter. "Mr. Paltrow, Ed Begley," I said as I waved hello. "I'm playing Victor Ehrlich."

"I know that," he said, and then (not to appear rude), "Hi." And he turned back to the others. "I'm just curious if I missed a rewrite along the way. Besides being a medical resident, is Ehrlich now also attending clown school, and that's why you have him in a clown outfit?"

Bob, the costumer, was a practical fellow, and happy to bail on his bold choice. "Bruce, we can lose the shirt. I just thought, he's from California . . . "

Mark Tinker was first to weigh in. "I like it. It's not the same old, same old."

Masius chimed in: "I agree. I think it's funny. In a good way."

Bruce now looked right at me and said: "Well, Ed . . . welcome to the show. I'm glad you get to see right away how my opinions are valued around here. They just spit in my face. I'm going back to my office, because I can see I'm not really needed here." And he was gone.

It's not just the shirt . . . he hates me.

Turns out I was wrong. Bruce became my biggest champion and closest friend for the six years that we would do that show.

And for the many years that followed, right up to the time of his death in 2002. It was the job that changed my life, and Bruce was the man who changed my life, and I am forever grateful for those six years and what they led to.

The writing every week, by John Masius, Tom Fontana, Mark Tinker, John Tinker, and Lydia Woodward.

The performances from Ed Flanders, Bill Daniels, Denzel Washington, David Morse, Christina Pickles, Alfre Woodard, Norman Lloyd, Bonnie Bartlett, and Helen Hunt inspired me and caused me to grow as an actor in ways that I could never have imagined.

I have never really been out of work since doing that show.

And the most important thing you need to know about my six years on that show is that it would have only been three, if I had gotten what I wanted.

Remember the part I originally auditioned for, Dr. Peter White, played by Terence Knox? That part lasted only three years after Dr. White was discovered to be the hospital rapist and was subsequently shot and killed by Ellen Bry.

Shot first in the balls . . . then the heart.

One of many times in my fifty-six years as an actor that what I wanted was greatly inferior to what I actually received.

History for the Pie

INGRID AND I HAD DRIVEN an hour and half to see our friends Malcolm and Mary in Ojai, and the drive was even more beautiful than I remembered.

Especially if you took the back way via Highway 126, a scenic two-lane road that cuts through Fillmore and Santa Paula, then finally down the Dennison Grade into the Ojai Valley.

This was 1984, and Ojai was a sleepy town of about seven thousand people, and it's roughly the same today. The smell of orange blossoms in the air. Clear skies above. Clear waters below.

It was a delight to get an invite from these two. As you might recall from an earlier chapter, I worked on Mary Steenburgen's first film, *Goin' South*, in 1977. But I had also worked with Malcolm MacDowell on *Cat People* in 1981, and Ingrid and I both loved spending time with this fun couple.

Mary is not only an accomplished Academy Award–winning actress but also an incredibly kind and gracious lady from Little Rock.

Malcolm MacDowell is a wonderful actor but also a glorious and fun provocateur who spent countless hours finding new and inventive ways to wind me up.

And like the many evenings I've spent with my dear friends Don Rickles and Dabney Coleman, I found it impossible to get angry when attacked . . . it was always so damn funny.

But for now, he and Mary had asked us up for dinner and later invited us to spend the night. They didn't have to twist our arms, as their home was as lovely as the town.

They lived in what was an old coach house, hearkening back to a time when normal passage to this farming community was done by stagecoach.

And to make the trip even more appealing, we played a game of Trivial Pursuit after dinner. A game I was well-known for playing. Johnny Carson would sometimes try to stump me with a question or two, live on *The Tonight Show*.

The show 20/20 once devoted a whole segment to it in our home. But this night at Malcolm and Mary's was just great food and great fun.

The next morning they did something quite unexpected. They had their friend and real estate agent, Larry Wilde, pop round and show us some houses that were available for rental or purchase. I suppose it wasn't that odd . . . I had remarked to Ingrid over dinner and games: "I could live here. Could you live here?"

It's important to note that Ingrid and I had considered moving out of L.A. many times. Not just the aborted Atlanta move that we discussed prior to getting *St. Elsewhere*. We had, several times since, found ourselves questioning the merits of living in L.A.

While driving our daughter Amanda and a car full of six-year-olds home from school, Ingrid had been hit from behind and had her purse taken, followed by some scary remarks from the assailants.

Jeff Goldblum got held up at gunpoint on my front lawn. And then there was the unfortunate business of me getting stabbed and beaten while waiting for a bus on Western Avenue. (More on that later.)

So a relo had been discussed more than once, but Atlanta seemed too far. These days I was lobbying for somewhere a good deal closer . . . say an hour and a half away?

Keep in mind that *St. Elsewhere* was an ensemble cast of about a dozen actors, so it was nearly impossible to be called in to work five days a week. Three or four days a week was the norm.

If we did move to Ojai, I could drive into L.A. a few days a week, and spend my weekends and days off in a more bucolic setting, which my family would enjoy in Ojai 24/7.

So, bold as it was to have a real estate agent friend drop by that day, Ingrid and I were actually more ready for a change than we knew at the time.

Larry probably showed us three or four properties, but none could compare with the first one we saw. It felt large for us at 2,500 square feet, as we were still living in our 1,700-square-foot starter home. But the property itself was magical.

A beautiful arbor, rich with bougainvillea. Twenty mature citrus trees, twenty mature avocado trees. A pool and a guesthouse. Plenty of room for my veggie garden. Bashert. It was meant to be. I asked my dear friend and cousin Tim Begley to handle the transaction, and he quickly learned that it would not be easy, as the lender had taken possession of the property, and foreclosure sales can take a while.

We were willing to wait. We both felt that this was our dream home. And it was one that we could afford, as I had begun filming my third season of *St. Elsewhere.*

I know I've explained that we were thinking of moving because of the danger we were all starting to feel, walking and driving in L.A., but there was another form of peril, posing an even greater threat to me and my family.

The dangerous business of dating one woman while you're actively married to another.

I loved Ingrid Begley, more than I had loved any woman who came before her, but—as I've mentioned—in my delusion, I actually believed that the simple act of putting the ring on my finger back in 1976 would *make* me monogamous, like some time-release better-angel dust.

Hang on . . . I gotta call bullshit right now as I write this.

Not because I just wrote "time-release better-angel dust." That deserves a severe reprimand in several other categories, but we can return to that later.

I call bullshit on the "simple act of putting the ring on my finger" whopper.

How would I ever know if that worked? I wore a ring for a few weeks after we were wed in Las Vegas in 1976 but soon convinced Ingrid that "I don't wear jewelry."

Which might have been true before we were wed (It was. I wore no rings or bracelets. I rarely wore a watch), but we were now eight years into a serious contractual relationship: licenses, vows, and everything, not to mention two children.

Take one for the team, and put on a goddamned ring!

What's so unusual is I had stopped drinking five years prior to this.

Now that I'm sober, why am I just trading one addiction for another? I was supposed to be practicing a program of rigorous honesty. How does that square with deceit on this scale? Deceit that I repeat (for the third time on these pages) made *me* feel shitty, too.

Sadly, I was not ready to give up this final addiction just yet. In so doing, I had surrendered to another good reason to move my wife and family an hour and a half from Los Angeles:

It's harder to get caught.

So, move we did. At first to a rental close to downtown Ojai, then finally to our own home on the east end of town, right in the middle of citrus, avocado, and olive groves.

We lived in that idyllic setting about four years, and *St. Elsewhere* kept getting renewed for season after season. We were doing so well that Steve Rhodes (Neil Rhodes's brother) found us a small home for sale in Studio City near the CBS-MTM lot.

Ingrid reasoned that we should have a comfortable place to stay when we all came into town. And if I had to work late, I would no longer feel cramped in my friend Neil's rental. Escrow closed quickly and my wife was soon in the process of remodeling.

Since *St. Elsewhere* was on hiatus, Ingrid decided that we would switch roles. I would stay in Ojai with our two wonderful children, Nicholas and Amanda. And she would sleep on a futon at the Studio City jobsite till completion.

But show business is a capricious endeavor. We soon learned there would be no other TV or film work during the St. Elsewhere hiatus, owing to the writer's strike of 1988. But how long could that last? I was actually quite content to stay home and play Mr. Mom with my offspring.

The project in L.A. kept dragging on, over time and over budget.

Then St. Elsewhere got canceled as the writer's strike raged on.

And Pierre, the gentleman who Ingrid hired to do the painting and other handywork around the house, kept finding new issues in that 1936 home that really needed to be addressed. Hey, we'd find the money.

I assume you all remember the "Ingrid's handyman" joke from a few chapters ago, so for me to make another childish joke like "Pierre was stirring more than the Dunn-Edwards" would be pointless.

And like several rooms in the house, paintless. He must have been distracted.

Okay, I had my fun twice now with my wife's boyfriend, but to set the record straight . . .

Pierre and I became quite friendly many years ago, and he is not only a talented composer but a perfectly good painter, so if there were any rooms unpainted, it was probably at my insistence.

I moved out of the house in Ojai a short time after that.

And let me jump far ahead and remind you that Ingrid and I weathered our divorce, and eventually became very close again.

Malcolm and Mary would split up, and she would marry my dear friend Ted Danson in 1995, and they have been in love and together ever since.

But before I close out this chapter, let me do so with a brief recollection of one particular memorable evening in Ojai with Malcolm and Mary when they were still a thing.

Mary often had friends from out of town stay in their beautiful guest room (like Ingrid and I had a few years prior), and the guests this evening were none other than the governor and first lady of Arkansas, her home state.

We were invited to join them for dinner, and afterward a game of Trivial Pursuit! After dinner, we split up into three teams. Malcolm and Mary. Bill and Hillary. And me and Ingrid.

After about an hour of play, Ingrid and I found ourselves in the "hub of the wheel," having earned all six "pieces of the pie" in History, Geography, Science & Nature, Entertainment, Sports & Leisure, and Art & Literature. The only category that remained was History, chosen by our opponents for the win, and it was a question about Pope Pius XII.

Being a former altar boy, I knew the answer, whatever the hell it was. But Bill and Hillary both contended it was something other than that. To which I responded, "That's what's on the card." They protested further but were fairly gracious in defeat.

And now the story really begins.

I saw Bill and Hillary many times after that. First, at the Democratic National Convention in 1988. I was a delegate for Michael Dukakis, and Bill gave a long but wonderful speech.

At Fran and Roger Diamond's house in 1992, I showed candidate Clinton and his wife their first modern electric car.

At gatherings over the years, large and small, where Hillary would often spot me and say something nice about my early electric car.

And Bill would, likewise, remember that day and that car.

But he would also remember that Trivial Pursuit defeat, and recount that it was about Pope Pius XII. And he would often supply me with what he felt was the correct answer.

Say what you will about him, the man has an incredible memory.

And he could be incredibly charming. He always made me and countless others feel like we were the only ones in the room.

I don't intend to talk much about politics in this book. I'm more interested in using these pages to find things we can agree on rather than find division in.

But I hope we can all agree that during his presidency:

We saw twenty-two million new jobs created.

We saw the highest home ownership in American history.

We saw the lowest unemployment in thirty years.

We saw a man who was a sex addict lie under oath and cause a great deal of harm to himself, to his wife, and to his country.

For my part, I had given up on the philandering, and the lying that went with it, by 1996.

I wish Bill had given it up, too . . . by 1996.

Things might have turned out differently.

Cryptocurrency

WHEN I FOUND MYSELF IN Manhattan in the nineties, I'd often dine at a lovely restaurant on the East Side called Nello on Madison Avenue.

I had just grabbed a quick bite and was headed out the door when I spotted my dear friend Tom Fontana dining with another gentleman. Tom was one of the top writers on *St. Elsewhere* and had gone on to write and produce *Oz* and *Homicide: Life on the Street* with great success.

As I approached his table, I could plainly see that the fellow seated with him was also a writer that I greatly admired . . . Mr. Dave Mamet.

He is, unexpectedly, quite funny. But I move to strike "unexpectedly" as quickly as I say it. *Lakeboat, Glengarry Glen Ross*, and *American Buffalo* are all wonderful dramatic works but also have really huge laughs sprinkled among the pathos.

And he is clearly, as advertised, a no-bullshit guy. I attempt to be a no-bullshit goy, and he responds by asking for my address, saying that he wants to send me something. I'm thinking, *A T-shirt? A newsletter?* If so, that's fine, because I'm happy to enroll in the Dave Mamet fan club.

He then decides to clarify and informs me that the package will contain "a little play I've written."

The next day I receive a copy of a play appropriately titled *The*

Cryptogram that is to be staged at the American Repertory Theater in Boston, and the role of Del is mine, if I want it.

My first thought was *I've got to send an appropriate gift to Tom Fontana for whatever lies he told Dave about me that day at Nello.* An armload of gold bullion seemed a good start.

That was actually my second thought, because Dave had included his phone number, so my first thought was to call and accept the offer, and I did.

I was to be housed at an apartment on Harvard Yard in Cambridge. There would be a five-week rehearsal period prior to the first preview. And the two other parts were to be played by Shelton Dane and Felicity Huffman.

The year was 1995, long before Felicity gained such acclaim for *Desperate Housewives* and *Transamerica*, for which she received an Oscar nomination.

But she had known Dave for many years and was a highly regarded member of the Atlantic Theater Company with other extremely talented folks like William H. Macy, a man who she would marry two years later.

Bill is a dear friend, and like my other friend, Harrison Ford, he is a much better actor and a much better carpenter than me.

Shelton Dane was eleven years old at the time, and he played Felicity's son.

I played her friend and neighbor, Del.

Having learned my lesson in the Strindberg play at Valley College, I dove into line memorization the next day.

Then I remembered that I had a few projects in L.A. to complete before I went to Boston, and I had to learn lines for those shows as well. And this was my first Mamet play, and I had not gotten used to that unique and wonderful rhythm yet. So when I left for Boston on January 1, 1995 . . . I had learned a whopping eight pages of dialogue.

I had much work to do, and I reasoned that once I got to my little apartment with no distractions, I could buckle down and commit to memory the other ninety-two pages of the play.

Did I mention . . . Dave is directing the play himself. And he's really hoping it does well in Boston, because if it does, they have the Westside Theatre picked out in New York.

No pressure.

To my credit, I got into Alan Watts *This Is It* mode and was completely present for the whole wonderful rehearsal process. I did not dwell on what the play might be on opening night, and certainly not what it might be in New York.

I loved every minute of those next five weeks of rehearsal.

As I did the previews.

As I did opening night in Boston.

As I did a few months later in New York.

As I did when Felicity won the Obie Award for her work in that fine play. An accolade she richly deserved.

To get the call to be in one of his wonderful projects is always an incredible gift. One I have been the grateful recipient of many times since 1995.

I got to do *The Cryptogram* again in Los Angeles in 1999, in tandem with *The Old Neighborhood*, another fine work of his.

I did a radio play of Dave's *Faust* adaptation a few years after that, and a terrific play called *Romance* at the Mark Taper Forum in Los Angeles in 2005, and I've never gotten bigger laughs, before or since.

I got to do *Duck Variations* at the Kirk Douglas Theatre in 2008.

In 2011 I worked with Felicity again on *November,* a very funny play by Dave that we did at the Taper.

A month or two before I wrote these very words, I did a staged reading of a piece that Dave has been working on that I hope I get to see, or even better, be in.

That lucky day at Nello in New York proves (once again) that I might only have, and I apparently only need . . . one talent.

I'm at the right place at the right time.

Coal Man

AS I'VE MENTIONED MORE THAN once, I worked on a show called *Mary Hartman, Mary Hartman* in 1976, playing Steve, the deaf boyfriend of Cathy, Mary Hartman's sister.

I was single when I started on the show but got married in October of that year, and I had completed all my episodes earlier in that same year.

Norman Lear produced that wonderful show, and at this point he had already given me some nice roles in *Maude* with Bea Arthur, and *Year at the Top* with Mickey Rooney and Paul Shaffer a bit later.

Years later, Norman's wife Lyn, along with Cindy and Alan Horn, would start a nonprofit called the Environmental Media Association (EMA), a group dedicated to protecting the environment.

But this was still the late seventies, and I was now not only married but had a child on the way, so I was really desperate to find work. I had taken a few stills of the cast during my time at *Mary Hartman*, and Barbara Brogliatti, the head of PR for Norman's company, asked if she could use those stills, and I of course obliged.

Then a wonderful thing happened. Even though there was no acting work for me at that precise moment, Norman knew I had a new family, and he asked Barbara to throw some work my way as a photographer.

Extremely generous, as Norman has always been with me.

But as it turns out, there was another bonus headed my way. While shooting stills on the set of *Forever Fernwood*, I was introduced to an incredible actor named Dabney Coleman.

Forever Fernwood was a spin-off of *Mary Hartman*, and it starred a good many of the original cast, like Dabney Coleman, in the role of Merle Jeeter.

He was paired with the equally brilliant Marian Mercer, and any scene that they were in was flawless and funny. And Dabney's approach to comedy was different from most folks working in TV and films at that time. Different in that I never once could spot him playing Merle Jeeter for laughs.

He approached this role in *Forever Fernwood* the same way he approached his many other roles that preceded it, in shows like *The Fugitive* and *Ben Casey*. He might as well have been doing Strindberg. He was dead serious at every turn, and it was always brilliantly funny.

I was shameless in my pursuit of Dabney, and he couldn't have been more friendly and inclusive.

Until our second dinner together, when he came after me viciously and relentlessly. As my other friend with similar skills had done for years, Don Rickles.

But with both of them, it was impossible to be offended, as it was always lightning fast and wicked funny.

I have tried in vain to "get" Dabney over five decades, and have never once been successful, even when I had some help.

The year was 1984.

Dabney was into year two of *Buffalo Bill*, a very dark and very funny show, with Joanna Cassidy, Charlie Robinson, and a young and wonderful Geena Davis.

I was, likewise, enjoying a second season on *St. Elsewhere*, also on NBC.

The only thing you need to know is that it was nearly Christmas, and the network had just sent out their holiday gifts to all their network stars, and we were two of them.

You also need to know that we both shot on the CBS-MTM lot in

Studio City, and Dabney would certainly not be going home during lunch hour to his place in Brentwood, many miles away.

I sometimes did take lunch at home, and I had done just that on this particular day, only to find a really nice gift from NBC: a handheld Sony Watchman. A small TV.

By a stroke of luck, I also had plans to dine with Dabney that very evening after work, so my plan didn't trigger any suspicions with me calling him near the end of his lunch hour.

"Dabney?"

"Yo."

"I called Spago, and I got us a table for four, like you asked, but I just wanted to make sure where you preferred to sit."

At this point, I slowly crept up the volume on my Sony device as Dabney responded, "Same as always, near the window."

Unlike now, we both had incredible hearing at this point, so he heard and asked: "Are you watching TV right now . . . while we're having a conversation? I'm hanging up."

"Hold on, hold on! I'm trying to find the volume knob! I just got my Christmas gift from NBC. This amazing handheld TV. I'm sure you got yours already," I said, knowing he had not. It was awaiting him at his home, as mine had been a few minutes before.

"Have you figured out the controls on this thing yet . . . Ah! There it is," I said, finally "discovering" how to turn it off.

Dabney stayed silent, so I jumped in, saying, "Wait a minute, now I feel like an asshole."

"That's because you are."

I pretended that I hadn't heard him. "Jay Michaels came on set and passed out these little TVs to the whole cast, was it yesterday? . . . Maybe a few days ago, and you're saying they didn't give you one? That's weird. I'm not sure what that means."

"Huh. They didn't give me a little TV," he said, sounding genuinely hurt. Mission accomplished! Got him!

But after a mere second:

"They gave me a really *big* TV. And I guess they figured I didn't need two, so . . . Hold on! There's a little trapdoor in back of my *big* TV . . . yeah, they put one of those little TVs in the back of the big one, I guess . . . as a spare? See you tonight, asshole."

And he was gone.

He was somehow on to me . . . again. I must have a "tell," even over the phone.

I gave up then and there. It was like trying to outdrink Shorty George Smith or Harry Nilsson. I was never going to beat a champion at their game. And Dabney has always been that, and more.

The only time I ever came close to "getting" him was during the many dinners we shared with our dear friends Peter Falk and Chuck Grodin.

I don't think any of us were ever truly victorious. But we were occasionally able to have him on the ropes, if we all ganged up on him.

We lost Peter back in 2011, and Chuck just last year. But I still talk to Dabney often, and I'm quite close to his four amazing children, Kelly, Randy, and Quincy and Meghan, all brilliant singers and musicians.

And my friendship with his family only underscores my takeaway after forty-five years of knowing and working with Dabney.

I've gotten so much more than I gave.

Hopefully, that will really piss him off when he reads this.

Sister Act

THOUGH I HAVE TWO WONDERFUL sisters, related by blood, I have had the extremely good fortune to have been embraced by some incredible women along the way with whom I do not share a specific genetic code.

You've already gotten an earful about my sister-for-life, Cindy Williams, but there is an even larger group of ladies who have been as close to me as Cindy and the Begley girls that you will soon meet.

And topping that list was Carrie Fisher.

Ours was a long friendship, as we first met when her mother, Debbie Reynolds, did a movie with my father, Ed Begley Sr., called *The Unsinkable Molly Brown* in 1964.

We lived in Van Nuys, she in Beverly Hills. And prior to working with Debbie, my dad had surprisingly few movie star friends. So when we were all invited over to Debbie's house for Christmas, I will admit to being quite starstruck.

Tammy and the Bachelor came out when I was eight, and I remembered that as being a big deal, as was *Singin' in the Rain*, so she still qualified as a movie star to me in the sixties.

And though she and Eddie Fisher had since split up, she was still with a very successful individual, Harry Karl, who owned a chain of shoe stores.

Not *that* successful, as it turned out. He soon lost all of his money and most of Debbie's in Las Vegas.

Little of that was known to me at the time. I was just awestruck by the house . . . and the pool! Two pools, really. One cascaded into the other. And as I surveyed this unimaginable extravagance, into the pool leapt two young children, Todd and Carrie.

Todd was six at the time, and Carrie was eight. So they had little interest in me or my sister, Allene, as we were fifteen and sixteen. So to them, we were roughly the same age as Harry Karl.

As I go back into the luxurious home, I spot Debbie going into the kitchen as she tells my dad, "Hold on, Ed . . . I've got gifts for your kids, too." She opens a large cardboard box and pulls out two transistor radios and says, "Merry Christmas!" as she hands us both a couple of Sonys. And she had *a case* of them.

Some perspective: The cost of semiconductors would soon drop precipitously, but in 1964, a transistor radio was still a very extravagant gift for a teen, certainly one you just met five minutes before.

I looked my father square in the eye and said, "Dad, ever thought of moving over the hill, so we could spend more time with these wonderful folks?"

Well, not so much said it as thought it. But I was sure I could make a case for it over time. Then I tried a different tack:

"Less smog than the Valley. Think of my blackened lungs . . . think of yours!"

Again, words I never uttered to my father, but he would surely see the wisdom of it on his own soon.

We saw Debbie and her kids occasionally, and then I lost track after my dad passed away in 1970. But I reconnected with Carrie a few years later because of her friendship with John Belushi, Jack Nicholson, Harrys Nilsson and Gittes, and of course . . . Penny Marshall.

This part of the story now really becomes a sister act, as Carrie and Penny became quite the dynamic duo in Hollywood and beyond.

They held their birthdays together, went with Paul Simon and Art

Garfunkel together, and were the best of friends for decades. When Penny and Artie split, Carrie had a cake made up with a rendering of a forlorn Penny atop the words "Troubled Water."

I knew Penny fairly well through Cindy Williams, so that only further enhanced my résumé with Carrie's posse, and then . . . a huge thing happened between Carrie and me.

She went into rehab and, knowing of my struggle with drugs and alcohol, elected to call me from a pay phone from the facility where she was in lockdown.

Our relationship then took a new and wonderful turn, and we became extremely close till the day she passed in 2016.

It was a tremendous loss for all her dear friends, but we have all stuck together: Bruce Wagner, Gavin de Becker, Dave Mirkin, Bev D'Angelo, and, of course, her very oldest and dearest friend, May Quigley.

Her decades-long friend Penny Marshall died two years later, and you should know that she was not only a great friend to Carrie but also to me.

She lobbied on my behalf that I play the role of Cindy's brother on *Laverne & Shirley*, which I wound up playing twice. And she gave me a nice part in *Renaissance Man* and was a good friend to me in so many ways.

Thankfully, we get to see Carrie continue on as we watch her beautiful daughter Billie grow and flourish as an actress and as a woman. And I feel exactly the same about Penny's wonderful daughter, Tracy.

Though most of us first became aware of Carrie's gift as an actress in movies like *Shampoo*, and then her iconic role of Princess Leia in *Star Wars*, her work as a writer would soon provide her a creative outlet that we as actors rarely enjoy.

Some degree of self-determination.

As hired hands at the mercy of so many factors beyond our control, a precious few discover another string to their bow, which can sometimes produce even more pleasing notes.

Carrie made just such a discovery at the age of thirty when she wrote her first book, *Postcards from the Edge*.

It was very well received and soon became a hit movie, with the expert assistance of her dear friends Mike Nichols and Meryl Streep.

She certainly continued to work and thrive as an actor, but there was no turning back, as she had a series of literary successes with *Surrender the Pink*, *Delusions of Grandma*, and *Wishful Drinking*.

I've tried my hand at writing a few times over the years, with limited success. But Carrie was unquestionably the one responsible for me attempting such an audacious turn.

I hope she had some small inkling of how much I loved and respected her.

I write these very words, and indeed this very book, because of her.

|||||||||||||||||||||||||||||||||||||||||||||||||||||||||||||

It was Memorial Day weekend in 1989. I was in Manhattan filming *She-Devil*, and I had just heard about a great new show at the Westside Theatre on 43rd Street.

The Westside is an off-Broadway house that would soon have great meaning for me, as I would appear in my first David Mamet play there a few years later.

But for now, it was running a show called *The Kathy & Mo Show*, and the buzz about it was quite good.

I have seen a few plays on and off Broadway in my life, but I have never seen anything like this. I laughed and cried so hard and so often, and I can't remember feeling that way about another show, before or since.

The show's various productions have been recorded for posterity (though, of course, a recording is not the same as the live show). So do yourself a favor and watch any one of them today.

If you have been more moved by a show that just made you howl with laughter, please tell me what it is, so I can amend my list.

The human-designing Angels, Sister-Woman-Sister, Madeline and Sylvia, Madeline and Michael. Mo Gaffney in the shower.

Characters and moments in a show that I believe did more for women's issues, LGBTQ issues, and overall acceptance of others than anything I can think of in the past thirty years.

They both went on to do important work in TV and films after that first very successful run at the Westside Theatre.

Kathy Najimy has starred in *Sister Act*, *Hocus Pocus*, and *Rat Race*.

Mo can be seen in many episodes of the hit show *Absolutely Fabulous* and the very funny film *Happy, Texas*.

I still see Mo often, since she lives in the neighborhood, but Kathy has moved to New York and is sorely missed by all who love her here in Los Angeles.

And . . . I became friends with Kathy's husband Dan Finnerty years ago, after we worked on a show called *Meego* with Bronson Pinchot, and Dan is not only a fine actor but has a group called the Dan Band that is an amazing evening of big laughs and incredible music.

I'm so grateful that I got to see *The Kathy & Mo Show* thirty-three years ago, starring those two comic geniuses and gifted dramatic actresses.

It literally changed me . . . and so many others. Definitely for the better.

|||||||||||||||||||||||||||||||||||||||||||||||||||||||||||||

I have made much of Cindy Williams and Harry Gittes introducing me to Jack Nicholson back in 1972.

While true, my standing in Jack Nicholson's wide circle of friends was surely elevated by my friendship with the beguiling Ms. Anjelica Huston.

The year was 1974, and Anjelica somehow felt I was worthy enough to date her dear friend Joan Buck, and I was more than enthusiastic about that possibility.

Joan was then, as she is now, an incredibly smart and successful author . . . and beautiful, to boot.

Though Joan has lived in New York for many years, I am always elated when she returns to L.A. for a visit and I get to spend time with her and Anjelica or one of our many mutual friends.

When I first met Jack, he was still dating Michelle Phillips, from the Mamas and the Papas. But when they split, it was Jack and Anjelica for years. And to me, they were the king and queen of show business.

I had a bit in common with Anjelica. Her father was of Irish descent and quite successful in movies, but the similarities ended there.

Besides being a gifted actor, Anjelica's father, John Huston, was also one of the most talented and respected directors in Hollywood . . . for nearly fifty years!

The Treasure of Sierra Madre, *The Maltese Falcon*, and *The Man Who Would Be King* are but a few of the film classics that he directed.

His acting work was breathtaking as well. The scene with him and Jack in *Chinatown* was more than memorable to me.

At one point in the brilliant Robert Towne script, John asks Jack, "Are you sleeping with my daughter, Mr. Gittes?" Roman Polanski probably didn't need to do much to help them both find their inner monologue in that exchange.

I started dating Joan Buck around the time that *Chinatown* was released, 1974, and I was inspired by Jack to try to get better at my chosen craft, so I returned to the great Peggy Feury, an acting teacher that I had studied with at the Strasberg Institute, and who is seated there next to me but my dear friend Anjelica.

It became clear in the first hour of Peggy's class that Anjelica had a far more serious work ethic regarding her craft than I did. And she took what she learned from Peggy and started to put it into practice in her early work.

She did a play called *Tamara* and received the great reviews she richly deserved.

And in films like *The Postman Always Rings Twice* and later in *Prizzi's Honor*, directed by her father. A film for which she won an Oscar for Best Supporting Actress.

A few years later, she was nominated again for *Enemies, A Love Story*, and then again, the very next year in *The Grifters* with the equally amazing Annette Bening, also nominated.

Anjelica would later work with and become best friends with another sister-for-life of mine by the name of Glenne Headly.

Anjelica directed Glenne in *Bastard Out of Carolina*, and they became thick as thieves during and after that.

Like Anjelica, Glenne and her husband Byron were the closest of friends to my wife Rachelle and me, and her passing in 2017 was a shock to us all. One that I have still not fully recovered from.

I was doing a series with Glenne at the time called *Future Man*, and we had no idea that she was even sick.

Drink in every moment, folks.

Any of us could go into "postproduction" at any time.

||||||||||||||||||||||||||||||||||||||||||||||||||||||||||||

As you just read in the previous chapter, my lifelong friendship with Dabney Coleman brought me to the set of a TV show called *Buffalo Bill* many times in 1982.

While I was there, it was great to spend time with other dear friends who worked on that landmark show: incredibly talented people like John Fiedler, Joanna Cassidy, and the brilliant writer Dennis Klein.

These were all friends that I had known for many years. But there was also an incredibly talented young lady who I met for the first time on that show, who had just appeared in *Tootsie* with Dabney, and though this was early in her career, it was clear that she was going places.

I'm speaking about my dear friend Geena Davis, of course. And not only was she great in both those aforementioned projects, she was the only cast member who also wrote an episode of that extraordinary show, and it was terrific.

I've had the extreme pleasure of working with her on several movies, and there is no one more present, more dedicated to the work, while somehow still being incredibly fun on set and off.

She would go on to star in *Beetlejuice, Thelma & Louise*, and *A League of Their Own*, and she won an Academy Award for her work in *The Accidental Tourist*.

She would perform many of her own dangerous stunts, become a crack shot with all manner of ordnance, master the sport of archery, and win a second Academy Award for her philanthropic work at the Geena Davis Institute on Gender in Media.

Nearly everyone I know, including me, was woefully unaware of the subtle bias that has gone on for many years. A bias that has led to a huge imbalance in the representation of women and girls in TV, films, and other media.

Founded in 2004, the Geena Davis Institute is the *only* global research-based organization working collaboratively within the entertainment industry to create gender balance, foster inclusion, and reduce negative stereotyping in family entertainment media.

In the eighteen years that Geena has been seeking to effect change, she has had incredible success in this vital effort, and she did it all in an extremely positive and inclusive way.

I've been incredibly lucky to have been present for two-thirds of her weddings and all of her landmark birthdays since 1982.

And to say that she has been a major influence in my life is to understate. I can't imagine anyone else getting me to go up in a hot-air balloon or participate in the far more dangerous act of line dancing.

And, most importantly, I feel a tremendous amount of gratitude for her influence in helping me grow and flourish as a man, by getting me to appreciate the powerful and influential women in my life.

Because that is exactly what she is.

Join us.

Go to seejane.org to learn more about this important work.

||||||||||||||||||||||||||||||||||||||||||||||||||||||||||||

I first met Cass Elliot at Harry Gittes's house in 1972, and met Michelle Phillips around that same time at Jack Nicholson's. But I had been around them both for years before that, given all of our mutual friends.

I remember being at the Troubadour in 1972, and the otherwise jaded crowd at that venue parted like the Red Sea when two of the most beautiful people we had ever seen, Jack Nicholson and Michelle Phillips, moseyed through on their way to the showroom to see Randy Newman. Hollywood glamour at its best.

Not long thereafter, I found myself at Harry Gittes's house on Beverly Drive, and who should drop by but Cass Elliot. The brilliant singer from the Mamas and the Papas.

Cass and I start chatting, and she somehow found me amusing, and took my number, and I took hers, and we promised to get together and do something, and boy, did she deliver.

I quickly became her "favorite askee" (her phrase) for any number of incredible evenings in Los Angeles.

Night one: "Do you want to join me for dinner with some friends?" was quickly revealed to be dinner with Jack Nicholson and Michelle Phillips.

Night two: "I thought we'd go see a movie" became . . . a ride in Jack's Mercedes to a theater in Westwood for the premiere of *The Concert for Bangladesh*.

Night three: "I have some friends playing at a theater downtown" was Joni Mitchell in concert at the Ahmanson. Her opening act? A newcomer named Jackson Browne.

The time that we spent together was amazing on so many levels, as she was one of the smartest ladies I have ever encountered, and that voice!

She sings with the angels now, and certainly did during her time here among us.

I have remained close with her daughter, Owen. And her granddaughter Zoe became great friends with my daughter Hayden years ago.

And though Cass passed in 1974, my relationship with her old friend and bandmate Michelle only got stronger over the many years that have gone by since those incredible early days.

Michelle asked Anjelica and me to be the godparents to her youngest child, Austin, in 1981. And we, of course, accepted.

Another wonderful connection with Michelle began in the sixties at an apartment on Normal Avenue in Los Angeles, near Los Angeles City College.

My first wife, Ingrid, was good friends with her sister, Russell, who lived there back in the sixties.

Russell has since passed, but she was as smart and beautiful as her sister, and that's saying a lot.

Ingrid and Michelle rediscovered each other after we got married and became extremely close.

They took trips together, raised kids together, and Michelle was even generous enough to offer her home to me and all of Ingrid's friends and family for Ingrid's memorial in 2006.

I talk to her and my godson Austin often. And I also know and love her older daughter, Chynna.

As everyone surely knows, Chynna got the talent gene from her parents and put it to good use with her friends Carnie Wilson and Wendy Wilson in the incredible trio Wilson Phillips.

Michelle and I are surely grateful for our success, but our children's success is somehow sweeter.

You'll hear more bragging about my offspring in a bit.

|||||||||||||||||||||||||||||||||||||||||||||||||||||||||||||

I have had an impressive list of heroic women in my life.

Jane Goodall, Dolores Huerta, and Vandana Shiva are the most well-known, and I cherish their guidance and wisdom to this day.

But there are two women not on that list who have had an even greater effect on me, and they are Allene Curto and Maureen Begley, my two real sisters.

Not that the ladies I spoke of earlier in this chapter are a fabrication. But these two are my blood sisters, and as such, they have the distinction of knowing me the longest.

Allene, my full sister, has known me since I was born, as she is eleven months older. The term that best describes children brought to term in such close proximity is *Irish twins*.

Maureen was born fifteen years after me and has a different mother: Helen Denver, Bob Denver's sister. Yes, my father married Gilligan's sister in 1964.

Let me begin with my older sister, as she has also shaped my life and my purpose more than any other person, living or dead, for these past seventy-three years.

She always got good grades, and I did not. But I can promise you that my grades would have been even worse without her help.

At sixteen, she became a member of Young Americans for Freedom (YAF), a conservative youth group; I tried to join, but they wouldn't have me.

At eighteen, she finally had the nerve to rebel against our father's political leanings and became a Democrat.

I did the same.

She was a devout Catholic who attended Catholic grade school and Catholic high school.

I not only did the same, I went all in and became an altar boy.

She saw the contradictions in that same Church, with regard to reproductive rights and poor people giving money to a church that was already wealthy beyond measure, and left the Church.

I did the same.

She moved up to Berkeley and became involved with the People's Park movement in the late sixties.

I . . . stayed home and watched it unfold from a safe distance on my TV.

Like I said, she's a hero . . . me, not so much.

My younger sister, Maureen, is a likewise courageous soul who has known her share of adversity.

My sister Allene and I thought we were the last of the Ed Begley "late in life" offspring, but Maureen proved that my dad was no quitter.

She was born prematurely at the Rotunda Hospital in Dublin. But not quite as prematurely as the math would dictate, given when Dad started dating his agent's secretary and when he got her pregnant.

Her name was Helen Jordan (née Denver), and she was a huge step up from Dorothy, the stepmother from 1961 to 1962, a twelve-month union that ended badly for everyone but Dorothy.

Near the end, Dorothy claimed my dad held her against a hot radiator, and that my sister and I locked her out of the house.

The latter was definitely not true, and the former almost certainly not true, as my sister and I would have heard some audible affirmation of one's flesh being burned.

But back to my father's current relationship with Helen.

She was a nice dose of normalcy, actually, and she already had a family: two boys and a girl. Chuck Jordan is a year older than me, and his brother Jerry was two years my junior. I just spoke to Chuck a few days ago, and we just lost Jerry Jordan three weeks before I wrote these words. Helen Jordan also had a daughter, Helen Jr., who was five years my senior, who passed away in 1988.

My sister Maureen had Down syndrome. But my father did not hide her away somewhere.

He took her on *The Tonight Show* with him and to any number of other shows and events. She loved to dance and had a memory that was as sharp as that of anyone I've ever met.

I, sadly, didn't learn that my stepmother Helen had passed till many months after the fact. And by the time I did, all means of contacting Maureen had become invalid.

But a few years later, I got a message through my website from one of Maureen's caregivers in Reno.

They had mistakenly been told that I had no interest in personal contact, but asked, "Could you please send Maureen a signed picture?"

I drove up to see her within twenty-four hours, and my other hero of a sister, Allene, soon offered to have Maureen come live with her in Springfield, Massachusetts, where she spent the rest of her very happy days as the grande dame of my sister's incredible circle of friends and family. As my good fortune would again dictate, I would have Maureen in my life nearly another decade, till she passed in 2009.

Allene works in financial aid at Springfield College and is regularly asked to speak at conferences around the country, drawing upon her many decades of making a college education possible for those in need.

Maureen was known and loved by all at those conferences, and folks still ask about her a decade and a half later.

And, as if all that were not enough, my sister Allene also found time to raise five wonderful children; Arwen, Aaron, Alicia, Andy, and Angela.

I know. Cut her some slack. She got a discount on monogrammed towels years ago, and chose their names to take advantage of the savings.

Allene and Maureen. Two powerful women, influencing me from an early age to act with love and kindness.

No wonder I've had such good fortune.

Idle Chatter

YOU'VE ALREADY HEARD HOW HARRY Nilsson introduced me to several of the Beatles, and a fun little calendar trick.

He would also provide an introduction to several members of another much revered group from that era: Monty Python.

It was 1976, our bicentennial year in America, and we hadn't been that successful in wresting ourselves free of British rule.

Certainly not with our music, as the charts were chockablock with songs from the UK. And about five years previous, we became deeply enamored with another manifestation of the British Invasion: comedy.

But for my money, not so much Benny Hill . . . it was really just Monty Python.

So imagine my surprise when Mr. Nilsson asked that I join him at the Navarro Hotel in Manhattan, and waiting with him in the lobby were not only the amazing Graham Chapman but also a comic genius by the name of Eric Idle.

Everyone I knew would basically be "off book," as in committed to memory, if asked to recite any of the brilliant routines from the album *And Now for Something Completely Different*. I can still recite much of it, to this day.

But Eric and Graham were now before me, and Harry was asking them something about the "Lumberjack" sketch, as he is soon to make

Python history by joining them onstage for that song, then promptly falling into the orchestra pit.

But that would happen days from now, and Harry stood before us, unbroken, but slightly tipsy, as was I. Graham, on the other hand, was totally in the bag and summoned us upstairs for more drinks.

I can't remember the exact details of who came up and when they left, but after a few drinks, it was just Graham and me, and I got to experience another first in my ongoing education, a passionate man-kiss from a Python.

I can recall my father and my uncle kissing me, but it was always on the cheek. So this was definitely my first man-kiss as an adult, and Graham moved right in and gave it to me on the mouth.

To my credit, I did not react poorly, as many of my pals from Van Nuys might have, by jumping up and saying something of a homophobic nature.

As I pulled away, I went so far as to give it a full and impartial hearing to see if there would be more of that in my future.

After analyzing it with an open mind, the answer turned out to be no, but it could have as easily been yes, and I might have moved to England and had a very different life.

Graham was really drunk that day, and I saw him several times after that, and he was sober each of those times. And so was I. He was extremely nice to me, so I always wondered if he remembered our little moment at the Navarro so many years ago.

I was quite sad to see Graham pass in 1989, but I would later have the good fortune to work with and befriend John Cleese and to pursue a friendship with the other Python that I met that day, Mr. Eric Idle.

Eric would soon move to America and marry a beautiful lady from Chicago, Tania Idle.

Eric and Tania were also friends with my dear pal Tom Scott, a great sax player, who played with Joni Mitchell for years, as well as my other pal, John Belushi, on tour with the Blues Brothers.

A few pages back, I spoke fondly of a woman that I had known since she was eight years old, a woman who brought together so many of her dear friends for laughter, food, and so much more, the lovely and talented Carrie Fisher.

I'm happy to report that this ragtag group of artists has not disbanded. We gather still, at Eric and Tania's, at Wendy and Peter Asher's, at Dave Mirkin and Savannah Brentnall's, and sometimes in my humble home, and we continue to eat, pray, and love our dear friends who are still with us.

Though the herd continues to thin, we still have each other. We still have today.

Alan Watts was right. This is it. Drink deep from the well of friendship, and cherish this moment . . . now.

Spare the Axe

I'VE CERTAINLY UTTERED THOSE WORDS more than once up in the redwoods, with Bonnie Raitt, Julia Butterfly Hill, and others, as we attempted to save some of the last old-growth forests in Northern California.

But in 2010, I found myself involved in a very different kind of effort to spare the axe.

George Harrison was an acquaintance of mine, and I can assure you that he cared deeply about the environment, and even went so far as to speak in praise of the Monkey Wrench Gang one evening at Carrie Fisher's house.

For those unfamiliar with the reference, the *Monkey Wrench Gang* was a novel written by Edward Abbey that documented the work of a group of environmentalists of the same name. They had become so fed up with the status quo of ecological degradation that they began to take some fairly serious action.

As in cutting-down-billboards-serious action, or dam-removal-serious action. So I was both surprised and impressed that George knew that much about the environmental movement in America.

I met him several times with both Carrie and Eric Idle, and each time I saw him, he had new and inventive ideas about how we could make the changes that we needed to make.

Then, one day, he was gone.

Not truly gone, of course. We all mourned the loss of his physical being back in November 2001. But it quickly became less painful, knowing that his spirit would live on with his songs, his reverence for all living things, and his beautiful family.

And it is with his extraordinary family that this story really begins.

I got a call from a mutual friend that George's guitar, the Rosewood Telecaster, also known as the "Rooftop Concert" guitar, was being auctioned, and would I show up and bid on it for an anonymous bidder?

I put two and two together and figured it was probably for Olivia, his amazing widow, who I know and love, and I was elated to be an errand boy again for one of the Fab Four.

I've been to fund-raisers many times that held live auctions, but I had never been to a real auction, like the one I attended to secure a certain musical instrument at the Beverly Garland Hotel in Studio City.

I was given a paddle with a number, and my bidding parameters, as well as a phone number to call once the auction had ended.

I did it all as instructed, and as some of you might know, I was successful. I was the highest bidder, funds were released, and I was given full and complete possession of that historic guitar . . . for about three minutes.

At which time I wistfully handed it over to the appropriate parties, but I quickly felt tremendous gratitude that I got to play a very minor walk-on role in the story of the Beatles, once again. To spare George's guitar from falling into the wrong hands.

Once again, I felt like Forrest Gump, Chauncey Gardiner, and Zelig, all rolled into one.

And though my purchase of that guitar was known to one and all, given the public nature of such auctions, there was a more clandestine mission I was sent on in November 2001, in the last few days of George's amazing life among us.

I was once again an extremely willing errand boy who performed the simplest of tasks.

I was charged with picking up a bolt of silk, then delivering it to a home in Coldwater Canyon.

That's it.

That's literally all I did.

I played dumb, but I knew who it was for. And breathed not a word to anyone, till now.

That bolt of silk was fashioned into a small number of pillows that were surrounding and indeed propping up a loved one of a family I know.

A loved one who was in his final days among us.

And that has given his family great comfort and solace to this day.

A wise man I knew once said, "All things must pass."

But when I hear Dhani Harrison play that guitar that I briefly had my hands on, I must also say:

Here comes the son.

Reality Check

IT WAS 2006, AND RACHELLE and I had decided to do an unscripted show to provide a forum for the growing number of folks interested in a hot-button issue of that time, as it is today . . . the environment.

In trying to find a suitable name for the show, I thought it best that the title reflect the underlying theme, which was not "What's it like to be me?" But instead "What's it like to *live with* someone like me?" That someone, in this case, being Rachelle.

We considered a good many titles and finally settled on the simplest way to convey that message: *Living with Ed*.

But as hard as it is to believe, none of us really did a thorough investigation into what other results might be found with a search using the keywords *Living with Ed*.

If it doesn't jump out at you right away, go ahead and search . . . I'll wait.

Yeah.

I can assure you that condition is not remotely a problem for Rachelle and the man she loves . . . or for me, for that matter.

Which brings me to the creator of the show, Joe Brutsman.

I've known for years that my wife loves Joe Brutsman, but it's not remotely a problem, because I do, too.

Like me, Joe had a long-standing friendship with Marlon Brando, as he and Tony Peck wrote a movie that Marlon did in 1998 called *Free Money.*

But it was now 2006, and Joe Brutsman had finally gotten serious about something he and Rachelle had been brainstorming for some time.

They had been trying to find a way to build a show based on my very offbeat relationship with my wife, and more specifically, the *extremely* unusual way that we communicate with each other.

Let me be clear. Our brand of humor is not for everyone.

We would often leave a dinner party, having excoriated each other over the course of an evening, and on the way home, we would enjoy a pleasant conversation, but by the time we walked in the door, there would often be a message like this:

Dinner Host: Are you guys okay?

Dinner Hostess: Hey! We're both on speaker.

Host: We just wanted to be sure that you're okay.

Hostess: That you're *both* okay.

Host: Of course, that they're *both* okay. Why would you— See, now we're fighting! Call us when you get this.

Hostess: Call me separately, Rachelle. On my cell.

You get the idea. We enjoy an evening of fun and games, as Edward Albee might describe it, but as we're whistling on our way back to our car, our former friends are filing for divorce and deleting both our numbers.

To be fair, few of our friends really had that strong a reaction. Most just found it tedious, and deleted our numbers for other reasons.

But back to 2006, the year that Joe decided that it was finally time to capture all the joy and heartbreak of what it's like *Living with Ed.*

For those of you who missed this little bijou of a reality show, it was on HGTV for two years, then one additional year on Planet Green.

But to get to that stage, we decided we would first make a "sizzle reel," a term used to designate a roughly ten-minute teaser that will be used to get some hapless network exec to commit to an order of X amount of shows, all based on selling "the sizzle, not the steak."

Joe's cousin Bud Brutsman had a successful production house that produced *Overhaulin'* and other muscle car shows, so it should be an easy fit for a show about an aging hippie riding a bicycle, right?

Rachelle promised that it wouldn't take much time to shoot the sizzle reel, but when it came time to actually shoot all the footage that Joe needed to make a sale, they came at seven in the a.m., and finally left at eight in the p.m.

Less than thrilled, I waited till they finally walked out with the last of the equipment, and I turned to Rachelle and said, "No way. We are not doing this."

"Calm down," she reasoned. "It won't be like this when we actually shoot."

"You're right. It won't be like this at all, because it just took us thirteen hours straight to film a ten-minute sizzle. How are you at math? That's at least *three* thirteen-hour days to film just one episode!" I grabbed my checkbook and waved it in her face. "Call him up. I'll pay him back for every cent he spent on this sizzle. But I'm *not* doing this!"

"Can you just wait to see how it pieces together? This could be fun."

She eventually persuaded me to not bail, and I'm glad she did. The show was actually quite funny and charming, and:

Everyone got a reality check.

Weekly. For three years. Which allowed us to donate a lot of money to good causes.

And to build a LEED Platinum home.

But more importantly, we got hundreds of thousands of people to ride a bicycle, plant a garden, or try some energy-efficient lightbulbs . . . to do *something* that would make their lives greener and more affordable. And I couldn't be happier.

And Rachelle? I'm careful not to throw around words like *happiness* in discussing my efforts; I think I've been bumped up to *tolerable*.

It's a start.

These Eels Are Killing Me

MY EARS WERE HOT, MY heart racing, as I played the message again to see if perhaps I had heard it wrong.

"Ed, the Bagel . . . it's Branflakes. Call me at once. I've got a project I want to do with you. I have all the funding in place, distribution. Come up here, and let's talk about getting started."

And then, as if I didn't know who it was, he added, "It's Marlon."

Is this really happening? I had been friends with Marlon Brando for years, often going up to visit him on my bike. A steep ride from the Valley floor up to Mulholland Drive that I hoped would impress him, and it usually did.

I was welcome there often, as I figured out a key desire of Marlon's early on. Or, should I say, a key restriction.

He did not want to talk about show business.

He would quickly change the subject if you brought up acting, writing, directing, dance, puppetry, Claymation, or trained seals.

He *did* want to talk about plumbing, electrical, drywall, straw bale housing, wind, or solar.

Yet here he was on a recording that I had listened to twice, telling me that he had a "project that he wanted to do with me." One for which he "already had the funding and distribution."

I left the bike in the garage that day, as I wanted to get up there and seal the deal before he changed his mind and asked Sean Penn to play the part.

I was up at his gate in minutes from my home in Studio City. And I knew the routine. But even if I had forgotten it, there was twelve-inch lettering on the garage to remind me:

STAY IN YOUR CAR & HONK YOUR HORN.

Absent the bicycle, I finally had a horn to honk, but I didn't. For I understood the purpose of such signage. It was a sensible warning for those who might be afraid of his two massive dogs, who were now approaching. Dogs that were large enough to compete in dressage.

Your best bet with dogs like that is to quickly make yourself appear supplicant and bow down as one might do when greeting royalty, even offering your neck as a sign of good faith.

Probably not the best move out on the Serengeti if a pack of wild dogs is approaching, but it worked with Marlon's dogs.

The dogs seemed happy to see me and gladly showed me the way. And I was always careful walking by the pool with these massive hounds. Too much roughhousing at the wrong moment, and you'd go right in the pool. And at this point in this pool's long history, it more resembled an algae pit.

Ah, if those gunite walls could talk . . .

Marlon was nearly dancing as he entered from his office, and he wasted no time.

"That was quick. Where's your helmet?"

"I drove up."

He feigned a heart attack before shouting to the other room: "Get me Patt Morrison at the *Times*. Major exposé, tomorrow's paper. Begley Bogus about Bike Riding."

Then he turned back to me. "I'll ruin you, then you'll have no choice but to do this project with me."

I let him have his fun, as it had the desired effect. We were both laughing, which we often did. When we both calmed down, he took a sip of tea and began: "Do you know how many volts an electric eel puts out?"

Hmm, wasn't where I thought we were headed with today's session, but I could usually supply him with an answer for such esoterica.

"Two or three hundred volts. But not a lot of current. A fraction of an amp."

Marlon smiled. "See, this is why you're useful. A good guess, and you're wrong, but not *too* wrong. Five hundred volts at about one full amp."

"So, five hundred watts," I offered, putting Pete Gibbons's class and Ohm's law to good use again.

"I'm getting thirty or forty of them. They should be arriving next week. Maybe you and Joe can go get them, from—" He stopped midsentence. "What's the name of that town down the coast?"

I was getting a little lost. I knew who Joe was, Joe Brutsman, my dear friend and producer, but I wondered, and quickly asked: "Wait, what are we getting thirty or forty of from down the coast?"

"Eels," he snapped. "Come on, the town down the coast . . . diving!"

"When you say down the coast," I asked carefully, "do you mean south of Santa Monica?"

He was growing impatient over what should be an easy Google Maps search . . . oh, wait, it didn't exist then. I strained to remember coastal cities. "Manhattan Beach, Long Beach . . . "

"Why are you still in L.A. County? I said south," he groaned.

"So like Huntington Beach, Seal Beach . . . "

"Now you're in Orange County . . . further south," he insisted.

Marlon grew up in Nebraska. I grew up here. I could do this.

"Del Mar, La Jolla . . . "

"La Jolla! That's it! The Scripps Institute in La Jolla. They're going to loan me twenty or thirty eels, and we can get started." He leaned back in his chair and studied me. "Do you know what a plecostomus is?"

My friend Neil Rhodes had an aquarium, so I *did* know what a plecostomus was.

"It's a suckermouth catfish. They keep the aquarium clean, by eating all the . . . "

I motioned out to his swimming pool.

"Algae."

"Okay," I said. "You've got twenty or thirty eels. The plecostomi are living off the algae."

Marlon was lying in wait for me. "And if you get enough of those and they start to reproduce, it'll soon be, as P. T. Barnum suggests . . . " He gestured that I could have the honor.

"A sucker born every minute," I said with great glee.

Now that we had shared not one but two big laughs together, I felt that this might be a good time to get back to his phone call. "So when you left me a message . . . "

He acted like he hadn't heard me as he spoke of a higher purpose. "We're talking about unlimited power to every home in America, clean and renewable, and it works rain or shine . . . "

As he droned on, I finally heard those key words I had so misunderstood: " . . . project with you . . . funding in place . . . distribution . . . " and I realized my dream of acting with Marlon would have to wait while we saved the world with . . . "electric eels?"

It was time to morph my disappointment into healthy skepticism. "How do your twenty or thirty electric eels translate into usable power?" I queried.

"You said yourself . . . five hundred watts per eel!"

I was not about to surrender easily. "That's five hundred watts measured right at the tail for a fraction of a second. How do you intend—"

He breathed a deep and weary sigh. "Here we go!"

I was undeterred. "How do you intend to harness said power? *Harness* being an appropriate term in this setting. Is each eel going to wear a little harness, like a cartoon seahorse, wires twisted to shit in the first five minutes?"

He lived for this kind of back-and-forth. "Would you please stop. There's no wires going to the eel! You put an anode and a cathode in the water . . . " He demonstrated with two spoons and his herbal tea, then added: "Stop being such a child."

"Okay, let's look at it from a child's perspective. You're not going to have enough current to light up a child's lightbulb project at a science fair, even if you have a hundred eels," I scoffed.

"You're always so negative."

"Like an anode?" I offered, trying to lighten the mood, as we both needed to turn down the heat. It worked. At least we were both smiling again.

To that end, I agreed to contact my dear friends Bob and Bill Meistrell, identical twins who had worked on *Sea Hunt* with Lloyd Bridges and were expert in all matters aquatic.

The truth is, Marlon was actually the holder of many patents and was never short on bold new ideas. He was quite skillful on the congas, and he held a patent for one-touch tuning on the drum head. Like a timpani drum, but for the conga.

And he had lots of ideas and several patents on energy-related matters.

One day, months after the electric eel brainstorm, he asked if I still had my wind turbine in the California desert, part of a larger wind farm.

"Yeah. I've had it since 1985. I'm still getting checks every quarter," I boasted.

"Mm-hm," he said, and then inspected his nails briefly: "How would you like to increase the efficiency of said wind turbine by . . . one hundred percent?" He let that sink in as he studied me.

"That's quite a bump. How do you propose to do that?"

He quickly drew a quick sketch of my wind turbine, now dwarfed by what could only described as a huge kitchen funnel, or a metallic cornucopia, or wait . . . was it an ear trumpet?

"I'm sorry, what's the scale here, in relation to my wind turbine? Is that funnel thing in the foreground?" I asked.

"No, it's to scale," he countered. "What's the problem?"

I suddenly felt like Anjelica Huston in *Spinal Tap* as she points out the confusion over the Stonehenge measurements.

"Can you grab that ruler?" I asked in the nicest voice I could manage. He reached behind him and presented me one.

"That's what I was afraid of," I continued as I measured. "In your drawing, you have my tower height drawn to be a full . . . two inches, and your device is *four* inches. Since my tower is in fact seventy-five feet tall . . . that would put your device, and I'm sorry to take all the fun out of funnel, but it puts your height at one hundred fifty feet."

He tried to interject. I went on. "Made out of what, by the way?"

"Space-age polymers," he offered.

"A fortune," I explained, "no matter what the materials. And the Audubon Society's going to shut you down as you suck up every bird in the Pacific Flyway and feed them through your Cuisinart."

He tried to stop me. "Why is—"

I went on. "I saved the best for last. Irrespective of those other problems, my turbine, and the concrete pad it sits on, is only designed for a certain range of wind. They shut them down when the wind gets too strong. This thing," I said, returning his drawing, "would turn it to shrapnel."

He liked it when you challenged him, but I was afraid I had gone too far again.

After studying me, as one would an ancient rune, he finally asked, "Why is it always no with you?"

But everything was not always no with me. There was an invention of his that made up for all the eels and funnels.

Deep ocean water cooling.

It's widely known that Marlon had an island property in Tahiti that he purchased while filming *Mutiny on the Bounty*.

Marlon and his friend Dr. Craven solved a problem that has plagued many island resorts for some time. Electricity is often super expensive there. Most of it is generated by diesel fuel that is brought in on diesel ships over long distances . . . you get the idea.

Suddenly a kilowatt-hour can wind up north of fifty cents. For those of you who don't look at your electric bill . . . that's a lot.

But there's a huge opportunity for saving substantial sums of money, since two-thirds of said resort electric bill is used to cool the guests and the employees, and to refrigerate the food that is served to all.

What if you perform all three tasks with the water that is right there at your shore?

Enter deep ocean water cooling. A pipe is run down to a fairly modest depth of five hundred feet. The temperature at that depth is around 40 degrees Fahrenheit. Which is cool enough to do most of the work in cooling said people and poi.

The water is returned to the same depth from which it was taken, and only a few degrees warmer, so it's not scalding any ocean creatures.

And it only uses a modest amount of electricity, because it is using the siphon effect. Or more like a funicular. The weight of the water being pulled up is offset by the weight of the water descending.

This promising technology is in use today.

And I'm forever honored and grateful that he and his family asked me to be on the board of the Tetiaroa Society, a nonprofit dedicated to protecting the environment at Marlon's island of the same name, and around the world.

To that end, the Brando resort was built to the highest environmental standard possible and, as of this writing, is hosting a global sustainability conference in the hope of finding new and inventive ways to address some of the most pressing environmental problems that we face today.

She Angel

WHEN I FIRST GOT THE news, I thought I was being punked... again.

I had already been the butt of an elaborate hoax on *TV's Bloopers and Practical Jokes.*

So if I was being set up again, this one was even more elaborate and expensive, as it involved first-class airfare and fancy hotels in New York.

And it was April 1, so I couldn't rule it out.

I dreaded the moment when Dick Clark came out from behind the mirrored partition and everyone had a big laugh.

"Ed, be honest. Did you *really* believe that you were going to star in a movie with Meryl and Roseanne?"

Whatever the case, I sat at the table with a script set before me, ready to begin the table read of a little rondo called *She-Devil.*

And in she walked, looking even more stunning in person. I was now in the same room, seated at the same table, as Ms. Meryl Streep.

To say that the lady is powerful is to understate. Like calling the SoFi Stadium roomy or the Pacific Ocean wet.

Which my palms were at this point, so I dried them on my pants before I shook her hand. Was I actually trembling? I was thirty-nine years old, and I was trembling.

Her other co-star, Roseanne Barr, seemed likewise thrilled to be in a room with her, as did Linda Hunt and Sylvia Miles. For her part, Meryl was somehow grand, folksy, scholarly, and sexy.

And it's not just her acting career that is impressive to me. She took a brave and controversial stand against a toxic landscaping chemical known as daminozide (Alar) in 1988. It should not have been considered controversial, as Alar did absolutely nothing to nourish a tree or its fruit, ward off any pests, or prevent mildew or fungus.

It simply made the fruits look more uniform.

Did I mention that it was toxic?

So Al Meyerhoff and my other friends at the Natural Resources Defense Council (NRDC) mounted a campaign to ban Alar, and wisely enlisted the help of an extremely smart and well-spoken mother of three: Meryl Streep.

She testified before Congress and spoke of it eloquently in the media, and very soon thereafter, Alar was banned.

There was a backlash, as there often is when going against a big company like Uniroyal, but she weathered it, and more importantly, the science did.

But now I was a mere three feet from her, reading my lines and hoping to get my heart rate under control. I got through the table read without embarrassing myself too much, and the director, Susan Seidelman, and the two stars seemed to tolerate me, so I wasn't fired on day one.

And I think I actually amused Meryl by forgoing the car they offered to return me to my hotel, and instead headed uptown on roller skates.

So far, so good.

I think it was day two of rehearsal that a suggestion was suddenly floated that might give us the fun button we needed for a scene.

It was the scene where Ruth (Roseanne) comes to Mary's (Meryl's) house and interrupts our amorous activities in the hot tub.

Ruth has a few lines, then turns and heads out the door, with me close behind, clad in only a towel.

That much had always been in the script and agreed to by all.

But this new request, coming directly from the troika of talent—our director and two female stars—was that in addition to exiting the hot tub clad in a small towel, I would now *drop* that towel as Ruth pulls away.

I attempted some feeble pushback but was assured there would be no full frontal. So that surely made me more receptive.

And in addition, the wardrobe department would fit me with an unobtrusive bit of tan fabric that should save me any embarrassment in front of cast and crew when we actually filmed.

All was going swimmingly, and I use that term appropriately, because once we began to shoot the long scene that eventually led to me dropping the towel, I had to get in the hot tub with Meryl and film the scene that preceded it.

The one where we go for a swim.

We both are clothed—well, somewhat clothed. We have on those flesh-colored outfits that make it look like you're naked, if the bubbles they've added to the water are kept at the proper height.

And they were. That's not the problem. The problem is that I'm now no longer in a museum with Meryl, or in a car with Meryl. I'm now in a hot tub with the most attractive woman I've ever been paired with on-screen in my life.

I take that back. I can't restrict it to onscreen. It qualifies in many other categories, as well.

But let me be clear, nothing untoward occurred in that tub, or in any other scene together. She was 100 percent professional and 100 percent in love with another man. A brilliant sculptor named Don Gummer, who she had the extremely good taste to marry in 1978 and have four wonderful kids with.

One of whom I worked with: the very talented Mamie Gummer, who I had a lovely scene with in *Off the Map* in 2008.

I had been through this before. I wanted to marry Cindy Williams since we met on *Room 222*, but she was in love with another man, my friend Harry Gittes.

Still, Meryl's kindness to me, and her tolerance of me and my obvious mad crush, are not to be soon forgotten.

We had lunch together, played Scrabble together, and played lots of wonderful music as I bored her to tears with my tales of being an opening act for many of the musicians at the Troubadour.

I am forever grateful to be a sort of opening act for Meryl and Roseanne in that fun bit of eighties dark comedy.

I have seen her several times since we finished that picture, often at the Oscars and other awards ceremonies, and she is always generous and kind to an old castmate.

The last time I saw her was at our mutual friend Carrie Fisher's memorial.

Meryl sang a slow and mournful version of "Happy Days Are Here Again," and I was not the only one moved to tears.

This was now 2016, a full thirty-seven years after she voiced her concern about the toxicity of Alar, and she had now become quite vocal about another toxic element that posed a grave danger while providing little benefit.

Our president-elect.

She has always stood on the side of what's right. And that's just another reason to love and respect her.

I am all the richer to have spent those few months with her, as well as her makeup and hair genius, Roy Helland, an extremely funny and brilliant artist who won an Oscar (quite deservedly) for *The Iron Lady*.

Roy would sometimes pay me a visit when he was in L.A. in the early nineties. And on one wonderful Saturday in late 1990, Roy came to my house for pancakes with a young actress I had not met.

But I knew she must be good.

She had just starred with my pal Harrison Ford in *Regarding Henry*, a film directed by the legendary Mike Nichols.

And I somehow convinced her to join me on a bike ride.

Forte Bening

THIS CHAPTER, LIKE THE ONE before it, is about gaining inspiration from those we get to work with and those we really get to know.

And in so doing, we sometimes find the ability to be a better actor, and perhaps even a better person. Annette Bening provided an example for me to improve on both fronts.

I'm not sure if I knew it at the time, but my invitations to go for a bike ride were something of an unconscious challenge for a new friend's strength and stamina.

And no one was ever able to make it up to Mulholland via Fryman Canyon without a dismount halfway to the top.

Until Annette.

I knew that she was a devoted practitioner of yoga, but I didn't know that it translated into the kind of endurance needed to ride this wall of a trail in the Santa Monica Mountains.

Think Lombard Street in San Francisco.

And when I think of Annette, I think of that very town. As that is the home to the prestigious American Conservatory Theater (ACT).

My dear friend Bill Molloy, surely the finest actor we had at Valley College, went on to ACT after his time with us, and I was duly impressed the many times I visited him there. My former co-star on St. Elsewhere,

Denzel Washington, studied at ACT, and he is one of the finest actors living today, in my humble opinion.

So I've always suspected that it was ACT where Annette got the training and the work ethic that she carries with her to this day.

And after working diligently at ACT, she found herself in New York and soon landed a starring role in *Coastal Disturbances*, the play that brought her such great attention in the New York theater scene.

But when I met Annette, she had moved to L.A. and had since done several important movies. But none of them were out yet, so I was not familiar with her work.

Boy, was I in for a treat! As was the moviegoing public. *The Grifters* came out after we had been dating for a few months, and I was totally blown away. I knew she was good, but I didn't know the full extent of her remarkable talent till that premiere.

I had the great honor of being with her when she received her first of many Academy Award nominations.

If there are any serious actors out there reading this book, do yourself a favor and watch her films, any of them. And you will see what happens when great natural talent meets incredible preparation.

American Beauty, *The Grifters*, *Bugsy*, and *Being Julia* are just a few that will inspire you to work harder and dig deeper.

I'm not sure if I'm capable of delivering a performance anything like her breathtaking work. But I do know that she has inspired me to work harder and do better.

And she is also a serious woman of great integrity. Since we had been together for that incredible moment of her nomination, she invited me to accompany her to the Oscars.

At some point, she must have realized that this invitation, made weeks prior to the Awards, would only complicate her life.

Then, as now, I refused to get into a limo like everyone else. The car I picked her up in was a Bradley Electric, an oddball kit car that had gull-wing doors and was nearly impossible to get in or out of, unless you were a yoga master, which fortunately she was.

But she had promised a friend that he could accompany her on that momentous occasion, and for a solid citizen like her, that meant something.

But her honoring that promise to attend the Oscars with me is extraordinary for another much more important reason. While she was working on the movie with the handsome and talented Warren Beatty, they both fell deeply in love, right around the time I developed a serious crush on her.

This was 1991, and I had not yet mastered the skill of realizing the depth of my feelings for someone *while I was actually dating them.*

But the truth is, it was easy to be happy for them both.

Warren has always been incredibly nice to me, and I've enjoyed his wit and wisdom at our mutual friend Jack's house over the years. And, I have long been a fan of his amazing career as an actor and a producer.

And thanks to Annette, I get to count myself as a dear and loyal friend to them both.

Dear and loyal friends who even included me in a staged reading of *Coastal Disturbances* recently, at a low time when I needed a boost.

Rachelle and I are always thrilled when we get to join them for a meal, or a momentous occasion.

Like my seventieth birthday in September 2019, shortly before the world changed in so many ways.

I thank them for their long and cherished friendship, and I say:

Put September 16, 2024, on your calendar. Ever the optimist . . . I predict a reason to celebrate!

Salad in My Underwear

IT WAS THE ARTIST ED Ruscha who introduced me to Carl Gottlieb and Allison Caine.

But it was sort of a reintroduction, as I had seen them more than once at the Tiffany Theater on the Sunset Strip in the late sixties, where I saw many hilarious evenings of improv with John Brent, Julie Payne, Rob Reiner, Garry Goodrow, and of course, Carl.

I should probably also mention that the Tiffany box office was managed by one Ingrid Taylor, to whom I would one day be wed.

Flash forward to 1976, when I made the wise decision of doing just that, and I quickly learn there are other benefits to this happy union.

Marrying Ingrid had given me the bona fides to be fully inducted into the inner circle of that brilliant improv troupe.

And besides the joy of socializing with all these wonderful artists, there would soon be employment in a cottage industry in its infancy called a Loop Group.

When I first heard the term, it was used to signify a group of improv actors that Carl and Allison had put together for a movie that Carl had written the screenplay for: *Jaws*. But not one of them would be seen on camera.

Steven Spielberg recognized early in his career that sound was half the experience in a motion picture, and he wanted to get it just right.

The origin of the term *looping* goes back decades. It involved an actual loop of audiotape that was played for an actor in a sound booth to replace some bad sound that was recorded during filming.

That could be an airplane overhead, a neighbor's lawn mower, or a creaky dolly track. It was something that you could hear on the original track that you did not want to hear on the final track.

If your line of dialogue was "The big ranchers are runnin' us all off," you would hear that line of "dirty" track played in your headphones till you got the pitch, volume, and pacing just right, and once recorded, that "clean" track was mixed into the final product.

Besides fixing dirty track, a movie like *Jaws* would also require canned background noise for a number of locations, like a dock, a beach, or a police station.

But Steven wanted everything to look and sound real, so instead of using "canned" track, he hired Carl and Allison's friends to come in and do some looping, which later became known as ADR, or automated dialogue replacement.

Though I didn't work on *Jaws* with that stellar group, I was called up for the next one, *Slapshot*. And I must have done something right, because I then worked on *Ordinary People*, *Coal Miner's Daughter*, *An Officer and a Gentleman*, and probably another hundred films and TV shows that I do not appear in, yet I am still counted in the acting category, as per my SAG union contract.

It's only an audio performance, but a performance just the same, so it qualifies for residual payments as well. Mailbox money. Thank you, Allison!

I have previously (and appropriately) given credit to Helena Kallianiotes, Arnold Schwarzenegger, Frank Gehry, Michael McKean, and Dave and Kathy Lander for keeping me employed as a photographer and a carpenter. And Carl and Allison gave me work not only in those categories but also in the new revenue stream of looping, as well as my first writing job on *The Smothers Brothers Comedy Hour* that Carl gave me years ago.

Suffice to say that Carl and Allison have been very good to me.

So let's go back to those early days at the Committee and hit the salad bar, where the brilliant John Brent served up some tasty fare that allowed me to grow further as an actor.

John Brent and another improv whiz (let's say Garry Goodrow, so I can get to the damn story) had originated a skit months before that was now a go-to "set piece," a performance that is mixed in with the pure improv over the course of the night.

But over time, this funny skit had gotten stale for both actors, and hence for the audience. Which did not escape the watchful eye of director Alan Meyerson, and he decided to cut the sketch.

Hearing of this, John made a reasonable request. "Can we take one more shot at it tonight? If it tanks, cut it, then physically cut *me* with a serrated knife."

Alan could never resist bold commitment like that and gave it the okay.

After Alan left, Garry asked John, "I'm with you; what's the new angle?" To which John responded, "I have no idea. I just don't want to have another scene cut, so I bought us some time." And with that, they went outside for a smoke.

They stood there for a while in silence, until John spotted something a few doors down from the theater and said, "Come on."

With Garry in tow, John headed over to a take-out joint on Sunset and ordered a small dinner salad to go, with clear instructions: "No dressing!"

Garry glanced at his watch. "You know we're on in two minutes, right?" John paid, grabbed the salad, and headed back to the theater. "Stay with me."

By the time they got settled in the wings, they had about a minute until their entrance, and Garry was getting worried. He pointed at John's salad.

"You going to eat that later, or do you intend to bring it onstage?"

"Onstage," said John, and then, "Drop your pants." Like the fine improv actor that he is, Garry committed to the gag and dropped trou.

John started stuffing raw greens into his own underwear, and equal amounts into Garry's, until the bag was empty, and they got their cue.

The only important thing that you need to know is that there was no dressing on this salad. So it was not moist enough to bleed through their pants and be seen by the audience. Nor was it an amount of salad that caused a comic bulge in their nether regions.

They performed the same skit as the night before, with the same lines, but this time with bigger laughs than they had ever gotten, because *they* knew they had salad in their underwear.

This was all a story told to me by someone from the Committee years ago, and I don't even know if it ever really happened, nor do I really care.

But I knew John Brent, and he spoke of the wisdom of finding that "salad in your underwear" that gave you that certain something that defied logic and description.

Finding that secret for a character usually yields greater benefits than the more traditional ways of preparing for a role.

And though there have been several bags of arugula missing from the catering truck on a number of projects I just completed, that doesn't prove anything.

I always sought out the most talented artists to work with, like my friends who performed with the Committee: Carl Gottlieb, Howard Hesseman, Rob Reiner, John, and Garry.

A practice that I had begun to rely on going back to my earliest days in college.

Kramer vs. Kramer

I JUMPED INTO ACTION THE moment that I heard the news.

Casting was to begin the following week for Tennessee Williams's *Summer and Smoke* at Valley College, and if I landed a part, I was determined to try something new.

Learn the lines, perhaps even give some thought to the character. Stuff like that . . . if I could find the time.

Just a few months before, I had crashed and burned in my vain attempt to bring Strindberg's *Creditors* to life in the Horseshoe Theater at Valley.

But I was told countless times that this was *exactly* where you were supposed to try new things and sometimes fail. A small theater, at a small college. Mission accomplished.

And when I say that I crashed and burned in *Creditors*, I'm not exaggerating.

I went onstage in that Strindberg three-hander totally unprepared, as in "didn't know all my lines" unprepared, and I thought I had gotten away with it.

Afterward, my friend Roger Reinhart had some kind words for my two fellow cast members and, in my delusion, I actually thought he was about to heap similar praise on me, but instead he turned to me and said, "And, Ed . . . you were there, too."

My neck suddenly got real hot, and I turned on my heel and sought refuge in the empty dressing room, then went farther into the dark and empty shower room and sat there and wept at the injustice that had just been dealt me.

For about one full minute.

Until I realized . . . it was like the search for the missing homework in Sister Killean's class. I was never going to find it because I hadn't done it. And here I was, in trouble again . . . because I hadn't done my homework.

I realized that Roger's comment was neither harsh nor unfair, and given the myriad ways that he could have described what he had just witnessed, he was being quite kind.

So I vowed I would never do that again, and I was now being offered a chance to remain true to my vow with *Summer and Smoke*, which was set for the much larger Main Stage and would probably be well-attended. And all that might even lure my father onto campus to see what his son was up to.

To be clear, I had no delusions about being cast in a lead role after my recent stunning defeat. So I set my sights on Archie Kramer, the young man who encounters Alma in the park at the end of the play.

It's a very manageable three-page scene and I quickly learned the lines. (Who knew it was this easy if you took the time?)

As I waited my turn to read for one of the lesser roles, I found myself mesmerized with the auditions for the male lead, John Buchanan Jr. Several of my friends at Valley auditioned for that part, but it is interesting to note that I can't remember one of them.

Probably because this quirky, charismatic fellow named Michael gave a reading that was very different from all the others.

I must have read well enough myself, as we were both cast in the play. But we were still in our late teens, so we were probably out of our depth in tackling a Tennessee Williams play.

This Michael fellow fared the best, as he actually had something going on under the surface that I don't recall seeing in any of the other cast members. And my depth at this point was measured in angstroms.

But before and after rehearsal, we were all transfixed by this new force of nature unleashed on us. And we even learned his full name: Michael Richards.

Forget Mario Savio or the SDS, we now had a new outside agitator on campus in 1968. One that would likewise get us on the floor, not as a sit-in, but because we were rolling on it.

We were soon introduced to Ernie, Dick, and about a dozen other characters in his repertoire that highlighted his versatility. Within a week, everyone in the hallways of the theater arts department was trying to do Michael, or Dick, or Ernie.

Summer and Smoke opened and closed, and didn't really change anyone's life, so Michael decided he would pursue more avant-garde material.

He did Megan Terry's *Keep Tightly Closed in a Cool Dry Place*, followed by *Waiting for Godot* with the very talented Frank Doubleday, who later appeared in *Escape from New York*, and Ebbe Roe Smith, who later wrote *Falling Down*.

Then Michael decided to include *me* in his antics one evening, and I somehow mostly kept up with him, but what happened next is something of a blur.

With very little preparation, Michael and I were given a slot at the Troubadour on Hoot Night, a weekly staple at that prestigious club every Monday night for decades.

Hoot Night was basically an open mic night at the Troub, and we went up and did fairly well for two people who had never heard of Viola Spolin, Del Close, or any number of books on improvisation.

Our opening bit featured two feuding pirates trying to broker a peace.

As a gesture of good faith, Michael would drink out of his imaginary goblet, then insist that I do the same.

I would decline, but with his imaginary sword at my neck, I would reluctantly drink.

Unsatisfied by that victory, Pirate Michael would then (fake) vomit into his goblet and insist that I drink again. This would instigate a violent fight that continued, even after we had dismembered each other.

Fairly sophomoric material, but it was 1969, and the crowd in attendance howled, so we were pleased. But we soon learned that Doug Weston, the owner of the Troubadour, had heard of our success on Hoot Night and had asked us to return and do another brief set, with Avery Schreiber watching.

Avery was a highly respected actor, having appeared in many films and TV shows as well as being a longtime member of Second City, a premier improv group worldwide, so he had notes for us, and good ones.

But you can probably imagine how much consideration two nineteen-year-olds gave to his worthy suggestions. As it turned out, we regularly violated every rule of improv that there was: "Never negate; it's always 'yes, and.' Establish the location. Try to find a 'button' for the scene."

We weren't ready to learn the basic rules, because we felt they didn't apply to us.

The comedians we most admired were rule-breakers. Richard Pryor, Jonathan Winters, Redd Foxx. They weren't saddled by any "rules," and they were doing just fine. And Doug Weston still felt that we were worthy enough as a comic duo that he offered us a management contract. Not an actual gig, mind you, but an offer to commission us to the tune of 20 percent on any and all employment.

Absent any meaningful offers or a reverence for the basic rules of improvisation, we never really got any traction, and while trying to figure out what we would do next, Michael finally found a "button" for our little scene.

He got drafted into the army.

He was (thankfully) stationed in Frankfurt and not the front lines. And it was there that the top brass got wind of his gift and partnered him with a talented African American actor and writer named Howard Ransom.

He and Michael were charged with writing and directing plays that dealt with two of the larger problems in the military at that time: drug abuse and poor race relations.

By February 1971, I realized Michael wasn't coming back anytime soon, and I moved to Colorado.

But my experience with Michael had given me the bug to do stand-up, so I wrote some new material and ventured out as a solo act, and got booked at a club called Tulagi in Boulder. My opening bit was a TV weatherman giving his catastrophic report while wearing a gas mask.

"Oil-bathers can expect some pretty nice breakers off the California coast. The 20-weight waves are quite nice, as well as the ever-popular multiviscosity beaches a bit farther south."

Followed by a commercial: "Now you can prepare a full tom turkey in the convenience of your toaster. Pop-and-Gobble! A tasty snack for young and old alike, it has the nutritional value of string, as well as being a mild diuretic."

Then L.A. beckoned. I got a call to do a Disney film, *Charley and the Angel* with Fred MacMurray and Kurt Russell. My plan was to come to L.A. for one week, then return to Boulder with a satchel full of Hollywood cash, and finally build my off-the-grid farm in the Rockies.

But the oddest thing happened: I got another job, and another, and another, and I soon realized that I had a volume of work that dictated that I move back to L.A. And no sooner did I do that than I got booked at the Ice House in Pasadena doing stand-up.

Then Michael returned home from Germany. He and I got an apartment together on Laurelwood in Studio City, and as proof that the timing was now right for us, we got our first gig!

It was a Fourth of July celebration in Burbank, and I think Michael's status as a veteran landed us the job. Unfortunately, we waited till the very last minute to prepare, which by now you've probably sensed was a major character defect of mine.

But we finally got inspired by a couple of cardboard refrigerator boxes near the dumpster behind our building. We got some markers and decorated the boxes to look like military ordnance. I brought a small tape deck that was cued up to play the Emerson, Lake & Palmer album *Tarkus*.

We came out onto the field in a Burbank city park, performed some mock combat, and at the appropriate point in the music, we both pulled out American flags and shouted something that I can't remember about godless communism.

Then I accidentally dropped my flag.

This was 1971, and letting a U.S. flag touch the ground was entirely the same as burning it. Especially in Burbank.

As the crowd turned quite angry and vocal, a man in military gear came out onto the field and quickly dispatched us to the parking lot, lest we become an integral part of the pyrotechnic display, along with our highly flammable boxes.

Undeterred, Michael and I appeared at the Comedy Store the first week that they were open.

Sammy Shore was running the club at that point, and his friend Rudy De Luca was his partner in club management. As you might recall, Rudy would go on to hire Michael and me both for the movie he wrote and directed, *Transylvania 6-5000*.

There wasn't much structure to our set, but we entered on roller skates while speaking in an unknown tongue and were outfitted in Greek dancer's skirts, so we received a much friendlier reception than we had in Burbank.

At some point during our roommate period, my agent called to see if I could make an audition for a voice-over job on an animated show. I replied in the affirmative, so he then asked that I demonstrate a voice that was appropriate for the role.

I did, and my agent seemed pleased, but after I hung up, I could see Michael pacing in the other room, and he looked upset.

Clueless, I asked, "What's the matter?"

"Are you serious?" was all that Michael could manage.

"You're gonna have to help me out here, what's going on?" I responded.

"What's going on? You just did Ernie for your agent. You stole my character!"

My response was both swift and credible. "You think you own all high-pitched nerd voices now?" We went back and forth on that one for a while, but he eventually relented, probably just to shut me up, but more likely because I *didn't* get the part.

But the truth I will now confess on these pages is . . . I *was* doing Ernie.

I had certainly done high-pitched nerd voices long before I met Michael, but if I am to be honest as I write this . . . I *was* definitely thinking of Ernie on that phone call with my agent.

I must have felt bad about that attempted theft, and my resultant cover-up, because a few days later I was hoping to put all that behind us, and I proposed a fun day together, just Michael and me. And I felt that the best way to heal the rift from earlier that week was a trip to Busch Gardens.

Located in nearby Van Nuys, they offered a tour of the brewery on a monorail that lasted about twenty minutes, another ten minutes of speechifying, and then the payoff: free beer on tap.

We tried to act like tourists to blend in, but the staff were eyeballing us from pretty early on, even more so after our fifth beer, which prompted Michael to reprimand me for not being better prepared for our role as tourists. "We should have brought some cameras, strollers, something."

"Cameras? Strollers?" I said. "What do you think that would cost? We could buy our own beer if we had a prop budget."

But it was all moot at this point, as a tour guide was descending on us with an arm extended to the exit while trying to make her "Thanks for visiting Busch Gardens" as nice as she could manage. As we headed home, I was the first to spot it.

About a quarter mile east of Busch Gardens on Roscoe sits a bar (still there) that on this day had a sign (not still there) that read "Pitcher of beer—$1.50."

Hard to pass up.

We pulled in and finally both opened up about some difficult matters. Michael shared about how traumatic it was to be part of the armed forces in what was still the Vietnam era. I shared with him a smidgen of the jealousy I had for his skill as a performer.

We sat there a couple of hours, opening up as we never had before—but also wanting to get the most out of those rock-bottom beer prices.

Satisfied on both counts, we decided to head home.

I somehow managed to surface-street us back to Studio City, and no sooner did we get inside than Michael drunkenly mumbles: "They taught me how to kill a man."

And I made the gross error of laughing, which was not very bright because . . .

(A) They probably *did* teach him that in basic.

(B) Anyone who did receive such training probably wouldn't take kindly to someone laughing about it.

And I was so drunk myself that I decided to double down with: "Okay, killer! Kill me!"

I don't remember any punching. It was mostly just grappling, and he did have me pinned pretty good several times, but I never passed out, if that was supposed to be the end game.

I finally caught a break when a concerned neighbor heard all this and started pounding on our door, calling out, "You okay in there?" By the time I opened the door and the neighbor got a look at both of us, it seemed clear what he was thinking: *Angry gay couple working it out.*

It took me many years before I realized how competitive I became with Michael, and how jealous I was of his gift. A gift he continued to nurture for years by studying films of the greats in physical comedy: Chaplin, Jacques Tati, Keaton, Harold Lloyd.

But by 1974, he and his wife Cass decided to move up to Olympia, Washington, to get away from the rat race in L.A. and were soon raising their daughter Sophia in a community with cleaner air and abundant open space.

They eventually moved back south, but not to L.A. They settled in San Diego, and try as he might, Michael could not surrender his love of performing.

I went to see him in A *Christmas Carol* at the San Diego Rep in 1978, and the play also featured a talented young lady named Whoopi Goldberg. They were both great, by the way.

Later that same year, Michael and Cass decided to move back to Los Angeles and give it another go.

Cass worked at Sears, and Michael drove a school bus for a while, but the Improv and the Comedy Store beckoned him back onstage, and I went to see Michael, and he was so good, I thought, *If he keeps doing shows at this level, he'll get an agent and get some work in a year, or less.* How about a lot less.

Within a few scant months, Michael was seen and signed by Charles Joffe, one of the top managers of comedians in the world, and he quickly got him a great job: a series called *Fridays* in 1979 with Larry David and Jack Burns, Avery Schreiber's partner.

So, though I wanted Michael to succeed, and quickly, I never thought it would actually happen this fast. And, if I'm honest about my feelings, I was more than a little jealous.

Also, 1980 was the year of the actors' strike, so nearly all the work that was available to me . . . was gone.

And Michael had a series.

To be clear, Michael was not a strike-breaker. *Fridays* was shot on videotape, and as such, it fell under the union banner of AFTRA, not SAG, who were the ones on strike.

When I finally stepped back and analyzed it, it seems like one of us was always successful, but never both of us at the same time.

When I had *Mary Hartman, Mary Hartman*, Michael was farming in Los Gatos.

When Michael had *Fridays*, I was putting up drywall.

When I was a regular on *St. Elsewhere*, Michael guested for a few episodes of the same show.

When Michael had *Seinfeld*, one of the most successful series in TV history, I was doing *Santa with Muscles* with Hulk Hogan.

I was playing the role of Archie Kramer with Michael the day we met; Michael would rise to international acclaim for playing the role of Cosmo Kramer on *Seinfeld*.

See how I got to Kramer vs. Kramer, there? I finally wised up and I stopped trying to compete with Michael years ago. I don't think he was ever trying to compete with me.

And I know I've found great peace in my life, as I write these words.

I hope Michael has, too.

Mother Superior

AROUND THE TIME THAT MY sister and I were born, our father's career was a nice mix of work on Broadway and work in TV and films. Consequently, we had the incredible luxury of living in not one but two homes.

One in Los Angeles, for the film and TV work. The other out on Long Island, for his work in the theater.

Though being bicoastal in the early fifties was surely a luxury, the homes themselves were anything but. Both had a modest two bedrooms and comprised a cozy 1,700 square feet. And they were certainly not in the Hamptons or Beverly Hills, but in the far more affordable towns of Merrick and Van Nuys.

Both towns had their pluses, and one of the best things about living in Merrick was its proximity to Manhattan. Less than an hour after boarding the Long Island Rail Road, you would find yourself in Midtown, an easy walk to the theater district and all the magic that that entailed.

One of my favorite destinations, once there, was the Lambs Club, a private club at 132 West 44th Street. And when I say a private club, I mean a men's club, and as a young man, that seemed just fine by me.

And it wasn't just me. Most folks felt men's clubs were swell in the fifties, and this opinion would not be challenged in any meaningful way for decades. The Lambs Club, which opened its doors to white men in 1873, only began welcoming women as members in 1974.

I'm not certain when they started admitting people of color to their rolls, but the archived photos don't paint a promising picture.

And in my own personal journey to treating women with the respect and dignity that they deserve, I had some incredible role models along the way, which you may recall from the "Sister Act" chapter.

But the role model who is the subject of this chapter entered my life at a time when things could have gone sideways for my sister and me, as we were sometimes put under questionable supervision.

Our aunt Bertha probably holds the top slot in that competition. She was once so drunk that Allene and I became the de facto caregivers as we struggled to lift her out of a ditch on Merrick Road near the Gables Theater.

It was around that same time that Allene and I had taken to carrying paring knives, and our father finally clocked that we were headed in the wrong direction. He contacted an agency and found a woman named Jeanette Pierre who came highly recommended, and Allene and I truly benefited from that good decision.

Our stepmother Amanda had passed away, or should I say our "misstep mother," as we had somehow missed the step in our lineage where Amanda wasn't really Mommy, but a page at NBC named Sandy was.

The truth is Jeanette became like a mother to Allene and me for the next five years. And they were key years, age seven to age twelve in my case. Years where you draw much of the map that will guide you for the remainder of your days.

And I can't imagine anyone providing better guidance than Jeanette Pierre.

She was from Alsace-Lorraine, on the border of France and Germany, and I'm not being overly dramatic to label her as part of the French Resistance. She hid her brother Charlie under the floorboards for years, as he had a higher profile than she did in the Resistance, and the Nazis wanted him bad.

To have sustained contact with a powerful and talented woman like her at this point of my existence changed my life and my sister's life in myriad ways.

None would deny that she was there receiving a salary, but it was soon clear that she was there for much more, and she quickly became this incredibly loving and powerful figure in our lives.

With Amanda now gone, and Sandy waiting to be discovered (along with my birth certificate), Jeanette became the closest thing to a mother that Allene and I would ever know.

And what a talented mom we now had.

She played the organ, painted, grew vegetables, and kept me and my sister in line. All the while making it clear that we were cared for and loved.

But what I found interesting to watch was how many men seemed threatened by Jeanette and her nonconformity to traditional gender expectations at that time.

She once went in to the hardware store in Merrick to order parts for a repair job in the basement, and the man at the register said he'd prefer to deal with the "man of the house." To which she replied, "I am the man of the house!" The owner overheard and sold her what she needed. She had no problem ordering parts after that.

But our need for education and growth was not restricted to gender issues. There were also many who had some unfortunate opinions on race.

There were garage mechanics, cops, and even some teachers who would sometimes use racial slurs to make their point or to spice up a joke.

Fortunately, there were a larger number of individuals that I knew and respected who *never* used that language. Starting with Jeanette. She had all seen firsthand where that leads, and she didn't want to go through that again.

She had strong allies among the Jewish families in the neighborhood who likewise did not tolerate such hateful words or actions against minorities.

Probably because *they were* that minority in Warsaw or Berlin before coming to Long Island or the San Fernando Valley.

We've seen where hateful words have taken us over the years.

It's not who we are and what we purport to be.

And I'm forever grateful to Jeanette Pierre and my neighbors in Merrick and Van Nuys for teaching me that at such an early age.

My Lucky Day

I WAS TEN WHEN I took my first cross-country trip on a plane. When we needed to get from New York to L.A., we spent either three days on a train or five days in a car, which is exactly what we were doing on this unusually hot day in 1960.

This was not my first drive across America in my father's Chevy. I had probably logged six cross-country drives with my father and my sister, and nearly as many trips by rail.

My father certainly knew that planes existed as a means of transit, but such was the province of movie stars, not the son of a hod carrier like him.

We were about halfway through our fifth and final day driving west on Route 66, and we had stopped to fill up the tank and purchase one of those burlap water bags that you hung on your car's radiator, essential in crossing Death Valley.

But besides selling gasoline and desert water bags, I could plainly see that this Nevada mini-mart had yet another revenue stream. One that probably netted them more hard cash than anything else they were offering . . . slots.

I had certainly heard of slot machines before this, but I had never been this close to one. And the idea that you could put in a coin, pull a handle, and win something called a "jackpot" was producing more dopamine than my tiny brain could handle.

I started fingering the quarters in my pocket as I neared one of the machines, and my heart was pounding. This was pure excitement . . . but also great risk, as these were quarters that I had actually earned.

I had a paper route delivering *Newsday* out on Long Island, so I had truly worked for this money. And, of course, that only added to the excitement.

But as I got a bit closer to this one particular slot that was clearly calling to me, I spotted a sign that said, "Must be 21 to play," at the same time that I clocked the coin purchase and redemption lady giving me the stink eye.

I turned and headed back to the car and somehow did the impossible. I convinced my father to go over to the slot machine and put in not one but four of my quarters, so that I could receive the windfall that was surely my destiny. This was no small task, as my father was not at all a gambling man.

And he did it, as I watched him through a glass partition.

He put the four quarters in, pulled the handle four times, turned to me, and gestured. "See!"

I just stood there, staring at the machine in disbelief.

My reaction, though completely illogical, was fairly sophisticated for a ten-year-old.

I was sure my father had somehow pocketed my four quarters while blocking the machine from my view. That he had pantomimed the whole thing to prevent me from winning.

An explanation that did not hold up to scrutiny for long. I had played charades many times with my father . . . he wasn't that good at pantomime.

So instead of just accepting that I had lost a buck, I decided that it was more likely that my dad had pulled a switcheroo to keep me from winning so he could teach me a lesson. Wisdom he probably wished he'd imparted to my older cousin (formerly brother) Tom, who lost a considerable fortune to cards and ponies.

My Lucky Day

I'm not certain how it was for Tom, but my certainty that I would win was based on a simple but deeply disturbed way of thinking. I thought the world . . . no, the universe, owed me.

All the while blissfully unaware of the fact that I had already won the lottery by being born Ed Begley's son. The term *white privilege* would not be known to me for another thirty years, but I was definitely already enjoying it.

I was only ten but already obsessed with slots, then roulette, then craps, and finally blackjack and poker. Just a few years later, at age fourteen, I would go to Builders Emporium in Van Nuys and buy the necessary supplies to build my own craps table.

I would likewise go to Valley Stationers in Sherman Oaks to purchase the felt pattern for said craps table, as well as my very own roulette wheel. A device that I used to bilk my classmates out of their pennies at Chaminade High in the San Fernando Valley.

That's probably the only time I consistently won a game of chance, as I was acting as "the house." Knowing I was not to be granted a gaming license any time soon, I returned to the other side of the table and read books on blackjack and poker, and occasionally had some big wins.

But for a compulsive gambler, every winning streak is inevitably followed by an even larger losing streak that causes you to do things you would not normally do.

Like taking a bus to Gardena with my roommate Paul Appleby over a decade later, thereby putting my life and his at risk, so I could feel the rush that only a game of poker could supply.

The date was February 17, 1972, and I had moved back to Los Angeles from Boulder, Colorado, and I didn't want to waste the fuel by driving or flying to Las Vegas, so I was starting to frequent the card clubs that were much closer than those in Nevada.

Like the Horseshoe Club in Gardena, California.

I didn't own a car at this point, but I wasn't about to let that stop me.

It was twenty-three miles. A long way, even by L.A. standards, so my roommate Paul offered to drive, but I talked him out if it, convincing him that taking the bus would be quite an adventure. And I did not disappoint.

The first leg of the journey went great. We lived at Vineland and Ventura Boulevard, in Studio City, which was an important nexus for mass transit at that time and remains so to this day.

I consulted my paper bus schedule and walked to the stop a few yards from our house, and after waiting only a minute, we boarded the 93 bus in Studio City, as it was running on time. We then hopped off at Western Avenue and Santa Monica Boulevard.

We waited just a few minutes to board the bus that runs south on Western Avenue . . . easy-peasy! The Horseshoe Club was *on* Western Avenue . . . I'm a genius.

But something unexpected occurred at Western and Imperial Highway. The driver called out, "End of the line!"

Paul and I looked at each other, confused. I finally spoke. "We're going all the way to Rosecrans."

"End of the line for the RTD bus. You gotta change to the Gardena bus line," he explained to us like we were a couple of idiots, which we were.

We did as we were told and exited the bus, and quickly found a sign to mark the stop for the Gardena bus system.

As two blonds from the Valley, we certainly stood out, but it was about two p.m., broad daylight, and heavily trafficked. "Should be here soon," I said to Paul, trying to convince myself.

What happened next occurred in slow motion and was quite surreal. Suddenly, there was a group of young men, perhaps ten of them, walking toward us with great purpose, and though it was five decades ago, I remember quite clearly what I was thinking: "They probably just want to talk to us. I don't want them to think I'm uptight."

Then a bomb went off on the back of my head, and I was down on the ground being kicked and punched.

Here's the funny thing about a group of people beating you. If they're also stabbing you, you can't feel that. That is, by comparison, more of a surgical procedure, compared to a full-on beatdown.

At some point, a car pulled up with two teachers from a nearby school. They had seen it while driving by, and as they jumped out, the young men scattered.

Paul had been stabbed as well, but he wisely didn't care about looking "uptight" and ran from the larger group, and fared better, as he had fewer assailants to deal with.

He also had less-serious stab wounds, as he had somehow kept his jacket on. My jacket was taken off instantly, so it enabled the knife to go deeper, and I wound up with a collapsed lung.

The police would later claim that taking an article of clothing was not uncommon, as it provided proof of the encounter. I had money on me, but the young men hadn't taken it, so perhaps that was the case.

But the search for possible motives was moved to the back burner as I grappled with my more immediate problem: my near inability to draw enough air into my remaining lung.

It's an unusual moment when you hear a siren blaring, and it keeps getting louder till you realize: "Oh, yeah, this one's coming for me!" I was taken to Centinela Valley Hospital, and they tended to my wounds and reinflated my lung. And since I was twenty-two years old, I healed quickly.

But the other kind of healing took a bit longer. There are many ways to process trauma like that. Some choose vengeance and hate. Others choose love and forgiveness.

I can promise I didn't transition my many feelings from the former to the latter because I'm a good person. I certainly wouldn't categorize myself as that back in 1972. That decision was made for purely selfish reasons.

I was doing it for me.

I somehow knew that if I kept even an ounce of hate in my heart, it would eat *me* alive, not them. The old notion of drinking poison and expecting the other guy to die.

I started this chapter talking about my lucky day, a term often used by compulsive gamblers like myself. It was that sick desire for the gambler's rush that put me in that dicey situation. It would prove to be my final frontier in my smorgasbord of addiction.

Would I come back for another helping, again and again? You bet!

No, *you* bet. I don't do that anymore.

My Lucky Day—Part II

I HAD LONG DREAMT OF getting a gig at the Ice House in Pasadena. And that dream had become a reality.

Bob Stane had taken to booking me there fairly regularly. And though it paid far less than film and television work, the money that I earned at small clubs like that was enough for a single guy with low rent to get by in 1973.

Bob had owned the club with his partner Willard Chilcott since 1960, and they booked the Smothers Brothers, Lily Tomlin, and scores of other name acts there over many years.

But as big a score as it was getting booked at the Ice House, I had also finally gotten a booking at the Troubadour!

I was to open for Dan Hicks and His Hot Licks, a great act in the seventies that would quickly sell out at a club like the Troubadour.

But it's probably best to focus on one job at a time, and for now I was quite happy to be onstage at the Ice House, performing as an opening act for the extremely talented Jennifer Warren. And that's exactly what I was doing on this Saturday night in February '73.

I would finish my first set at around eight thirty, and wasn't due back onstage till about ten o'clock. And I was actually contemplating doing something insane during those ninety minutes.

A casting director named Marvin Paige had invited me to his big Hollywood party, and I told him I'd drop by after my second set ended at ten thirty, which seemed to offend him slightly. So much so that he added, "Come earlier than that! There's going to be a lot of important industry people there. And some lovely ladies around your age."

I'll give Marvin the benefit of the doubt. Maybe he didn't know that the Ice House was in Pasadena, a full sixteen miles away from his little chateau in Tinseltown, but he *did* know how to pique my interest. Available ladies *and* a career move.

My focus moved from "Would I show up at this bash?" to "How can I get there and back between sets?" And that can be a tricky question for a man with my transportation history.

I had sold my electric car when I moved to Boulder, Colorado, as I certainly didn't need one in that small town. A bicycle was all that was needed during my time there.

But now that I had moved back to L.A., I found myself getting jobs at the Ice House and other locations beyond a bike ride, so I chose to compromise and buy a small car.

A Karmann Ghia, which was a fairly fuel-efficient vehicle of that day, and its speed and maneuverability would serve me well on this occasion.

I finished my set a bit early and I was out the door, heading west on Colorado Boulevard to the Pasadena Freeway, the first freeway in California. And no one who has even seen a picture of it doubts that fact.

It has only two lanes, and hairpin turns, and on- and off-ramps designed for a Model T, so there would be no zipping through traffic like the 405 or the 101. It was a few yards short of the on-ramp that the folly of this endeavor sank in.

I would never make it all the way to Hollywood and back in what was now eighty-five minutes.

I wisely decided to return to the Ice House and the job I was hired to do.

But it turns out each of those detours and changes of heart were essential to get me to that all-important intersection of Green Street and Raymond at precisely the right moment where destiny was patiently lying in wait.

It really didn't matter that the light was green for me and red for the '67 Olds as I entered the intersection. When a Karmann Ghia and an Olds square off, the little German dude doesn't stand a chance against the burly American.

He T-boned me pretty good, and my Karmann Ghia slid sideways until it finally came to rest up against a small tree. I remember being grateful that I didn't knock down that vulnerable sapling.

That gratitude was short-lived, as it was quickly overtaken by a pain in my left leg that I had never experienced before. The seriousness of the injury was also confirmed by a swelling in my leg that seemed to keep growing to an extent that I thought it would rip open my jeans.

I was taken to Huntington Memorial Hospital in Pasadena, where they informed me that I had a fractured femur. And to heal correctly, it would require six weeks in a hospital bed in traction. And if that went well, I might be released, but only by wearing a spica (full-body) cast for eight weeks.

Not only would I not be going back to the Ice House anytime soon, but I could also say goodbye to the Troubadour, Dan Hicks, and all manner of licks, hot or otherwise.

As the losses from this accident piled up, I could see that I had not merely shattered my femur. I had likewise broken my resolve to drive an electric car, or any small car, like the one I was in that night.

I would not drive for the next year, and when I did, it would be a Toyota Land Cruiser, as I reasoned that would afford me the extra protection that I thought I needed.

But, as you read earlier of that Christmas Eve on the Sunset Strip, my problems would transcend any guarantee of safety that I was searching for.

At some point during all this, the nurse gave me a rather robust painkiller. So potent that I hallucinated actress Annette O'Toole and Bruno Kirby's dad, Bruce, standing beside me in my room.

I soon realized that it was not an opiated dream when Bruno joined his girlfriend and his father and told them he'd stay with me for a while.

Another thing that occurred to me under heavy sedation was the date. It was February 17, 1973. The same exact day, a year later, as that unfortunate bus ride to Gardena and the events that followed.

Maybe it was the pain, the date, the morphine, I'm not certain. But I remember getting emotional with Bruno.

"I'm cursed! February 17, and every day!"

Bruno, ever circumspect, tried to reason with me. "I agree, it's weird, Eddie, but it's just a day, like any day—"

I cut him off. "A day like any other? Can you not see the timing involved? If I had just gotten there one second earlier or later, that Olds would have missed me by a mile! I'm cursed!"

Bruno always seemed to have sage wisdom at his fingertips, and tonight was no exception.

"I can see why you think that, Eddie, but forget huge chunks of time like a full second or two . . . if you'd hit that intersection just *one tenth* of a second earlier than you did, it wouldn't have been your femur that was broken, but your spinal cord, and we'd be having a very different conversation now."

As usual, Bruno was right. The orthopedic surgeon came in to talk to me and offered me the option of a new procedure that would shorten my time in the hospital.

"We open up your leg and join the broken pieces of the femur with a metal plate that will keep it rigid as it heals, and then we go back in a year later, when the bone is fully knitted, and remove the plate."

I told the doctor that I needed a minute.

I asked Bruno what he thought, and he thought that the plate was a good idea.

I shared some concerns. I told him I didn't want to "put anything foreign in my body."

Bruno, without a beat: "That's not what I heard about your stay in County Jail."

Always lightning fast and wicked funny. And extremely painful. Laughter at that level rattled the broken femur and caused me to both laugh and cry out in pain. Which, in itself, is pretty goddamn funny.

We went back and forth, laughter and pain, plate and no plate, and when the doctor returned, I told him, "No plate."

Allow me to flash forward about six months, and you'll see . . . Bruno was proven right again.

After six weeks in traction and eight weeks in a body cast . . . my femur did not heal straight.

Absent the plate, the orthopedist had somehow set the bone a full 15 degrees off.

All of which led to a host of problems with my left knee and ankle. Problems that I finally addressed in 1998 by having a surgeon rebreak my femur, remove the bone marrow, and insert a titanium rod down my now straightened leg.

No traction. No body cast. No damage to the knee like the fourteen weeks of immobility in traction and the cast.

More important than being right, Bruno eventually made me realize that I had been far more lucky than unlucky my whole life.

He demonstrated it in his life. Not by talk, but by his actions.

He came to visit me every day for the entire six weeks I was in traction in Pasadena. And he lived in Hollywood.

He brought me my mail, he went to my bank, he went to Erewhon and picked up healthy food so I could heal quickly . . . and I did.

Bruno was my role model every day of the thirty-five years that I knew him. I don't recall ever seeing him rush . . . anywhere. Always present, always generous. And always very accepting of what is.

Over time I realized that every single bit of that evening in Pasadena long ago was essential to me being this guy, in this chair right now, hitting these keys to convey this message:

Stop racing around trying to find it. You already have it.

And if you pass it on, you get to keep it.

The truth is, February 17 has always been my lucky day.

And so have the other 364.

Be grateful for it.

Then get to work.

Senior Moment

I HAVE HEAPED MUCH PRAISE on my father in this book, but I've also had a few "notes" for him as well.

I'm sure my offspring have a few for me, too.

But in the plus and minus of it all, his account is not overdrawn. He instead has a robust balance for one simple reason:

He did pretty well with what he was given.

I can only hope that my children can see the wisdom of such an assessment at some point in their lives.

There is much I don't know about his past, but there are many things I have learned since his passing that place him squarely in the black.

His parents came over on a boat from Ireland in 1897 and raised a family in Hartford, Connecticut. Michael was a hod carrier by trade, and Honoria Clifford stayed home and raised the kids: Mary, Helene, Ed, and Martin.

A hod carrier is the guy who schleps huge loads of bricks up a series of ladders so that the masons can lay them in place.

It is the very definition of heavy lifting.

My Aunt Mary died the year I was born, so I know little of her, but I knew Martin and Helene quite well, and my uncle Martin was, like my dad, highly regarded in television and films, as he worked for many years at Lennen & Newell Casting in Manhattan, and later at NBC.

I have heard from scores of actors over the years who credited my uncle Martin with giving them their big break.

My aunt Helene married a cop, Bill Falvey, and if she had an occupation before that union, I never knew of it.

But she holds a prominent place in my father's treasure trove of secrets and lies, as she got drunk one day at our home in Van Nuys and informed my brother Tom Begley that he was not really her nephew but in fact her son.

To this day, no one knows, or is willing to tell, who Tom's father is. We only know that my father raised him as his son, till his sister spilled the beans.

Another possible clue to the events that shaped my father's life is that he ran away from home when he was in third grade. It's a statement I believe to be true, as I heard him say it a hundred times, and it appears regularly in many clippings and documents.

As he told it, he ran away to join the circus, but . . . I believe third grade puts you at around eight years of age. Were kids allowed to just leave and join the circus at age eight back then?

I can't say for certain what was going on in a household where a child leaves home at that tender age, but it's probably not good.

A few years later, my father entered and won a Charlie Chaplin contest and got a taste for performing.

Unsure what to do next with that, he joined the navy, worked as a short-order cook, and eventually landed at the Wiremold plant in Hartford where he and his new bride, Amanda Huff, raised their only child, Tom . . . who was really their nephew. I visited the Wiremold plant many times, and always thought, *Is this what actors do when they're trying to break into the business?*

And I soon learned for myself that that is exactly what they do.

I worked at See's Candies and Orange Julius, had a paper route, worked at Inspection Service, and put up drywall for Frank Gehry, all the while in pursuit of a SAG card.

But back to Ed Sr. and his journey. He became part of the Guy Hedland Players in Hartford, then quickly began to work at WTIC, also in that fair city.

He went on to New York and made quite a name for himself in radio there, appearing in the hit shows of the day: *Richard Diamond, Private Detective, The Aldrich Family,* and countless others.

He was soon on Broadway in *All My Sons,* directed by Elia Kazan, and *Inherit the Wind,* for which he and Paul Muni both won Tony Awards.

All of which, impossibly, brings us to *Saturday Night Live.*

I had only done stand-up comedy for about a half-dozen years. But for most stand-up comics I know, the greatest moment in your career occurs when you are asked to host *Saturday Night Live.*

That incredible honor befell me in 1984, when I was two seasons into another NBC show . . . *St. Elsewhere.*

Lorne Michaels had stepped away from the show for a few years, and this was one of those years, and he was certainly missed, but the cast was stellar: Billy Crystal, Christopher Guest, Martin Short, Julia Louis-Dreyfus, Harry Shearer, Jim Belushi, and many more, onstage and in the writer's room.

The talented Brad Hall was a writer on the show that season, as was an extremely talented writer that I had met with Michael Richards when he was doing *Fridays* . . . Larry David.

A deep bench of writing and acting talent, if ever there was.

But back to Ed Begley Sr.

The savvy readers among us are surely thinking, *What is the connection with Ed Begley Sr. and SNL? The show premiered in 1975, and the elder Begley left us five years before.*

I'll explain. As I'm enjoying what is possibly the happiest week of my life, Dick Ebersol floats the idea that I could make a big announcement at the end of the opening monologue that "I am officially dropping the 'Junior' from my name from this point forward!"

They had a cute graphic that appeared to my side that had my name, and as I pushed the "Jr." down and away from "Ed Begley Jr." it was now gone, never to return.

A case could be made for that. I was now a thirty-five-year-old man. My father had been gone nearly a decade and a half. It was time to let all that go. And so I did.

Or so I thought.

It turns out there are very good rules about what name you are allowed to use when you join the Screen Actors Guild. You don't get to be Wally Cox, even if you are Wally Cox.

There was a very funny actor who had been working since I was born in 1949, and he was born Wally Cox, and he got to be Wally Cox till he passed in 1973. He was a talented fellow who starred in *Mister Peepers* and was also a very close friend of Marlon Brando's.

But there's another actor who was born Wally Cox. Yet we know him as the wonderful actor Bud Cort.

The elder Wally Cox walked into the SAG offices first and registered as Wally Cox in 1949.

The younger Wally Cox walked into the SAG offices in 1967 and was told, "Make another selection. That one's taken."

"Okay," he decided, "put me down for Bud Cort."

He could have done what my friend Bill Macy did. When the Bill Macy who married Felicity Huffman and was so brilliant in dozens of Mamet plays and dozens of movies walked into SAG in 1978 to join, my other pal Bill Macy (from the series *Maude* and many other fine works) had already parked in that slot.

Bill became William H. Macy in all matters SAG, which is likely his full legal name. All this is background to explain that my brief declaration on *SNL* was short-lived.

I don't get to be Ed Begley on *Saturday Night Live* or on *St. Elsewhere*. Nor should I.

I can be Ed Begley at the bank or the dry cleaners. But films and TV shows have a long archival life. And we should be able to look at the credits and know who's who.

Who won an Oscar and a Tony, and who did not.

I say this without an ounce of jealousy or rancor. Hey, I got to be governor for fifteen years!

Of the Academy of Motion Picture Arts and Sciences. I have had a long and wonderful life, separate from my father . . . but also *because* of my father.

I'm convinced, to this day, that had my dad been a plumber, I would probably still be fitting pipe and espousing the benefits of copper over galvanized steel.

I wanted to do what he did . . . and I'm still doing it! For considerably longer than him, so that's my award, and I'll take it.

I loved the old man while he was here among us, and continue to do so to this day.

See you soon, Pop . . . but not too soon.

The Governor's Race

MANY OF MY FRIENDS WERE beginning to voice their concern about the governor's race.

The power had been in the hands of older white men for so long, but now there was a call for real change, with a fervor that was growing by the day.

And I found myself in the middle of it.

For it was not just the governor's race that was being debated, but also the governor's gender. This will all make sense, I promise.

I had been a governor on the Academy board for a decade and a half, having first been elected in 2000. And for reasons I don't fully understand, I kept getting nominated and elected by the Actors Branch of that esteemed organization.

Let me not play dumb here. I was born at Hollywood Presbyterian Hospital in 1949. I am the son of a much-revered Academy Award–winning actor. I have been working in TV and films for fifty-six years. I know a lot of people.

It's probably a shorter list of people that I don't know.

There's a dolly grip at Disney, and a PR man at Paramount who I've never met. I'm going to take them both to lunch next week and clear that up.

But back to the Academy. It's not like there were *no* women on that illustrious board over the years. I had the honor of nominating and voting for Cheryl Boone Isaacs for both her terms as Academy president. And as far back as 1979, the brilliant Fay Kanin held that post.

But as the #OscarsSoWhite movement began to challenge the status quo, a spotlight was being shined on the demographics of the governing board and the larger membership in the Academy.

As an example, there were forty-three Academy governors in 2008, and only one of them was African American. Six were women.

A jaw-dropping discovery, really . . . when you consider the makeup of the film and TV business at large, which at the time was . . . pretty much the same.

Which brings us to the Academy Board of Governors election of 2016. I had vowed that I would not run again, as I had served for fifteen years, and it was time to step aside and make way for more of a gender balance on the board, as well as being more inclusive toward people of color.

But then I made a huge mistake with my mobile phone while in the recovery room at UCLA, having just had a sleep apnea device implanted in my chest.

Actually, two mistakes. One was answering my phone while under heavy sedation. The other was having a sleep apnea device implanted in my chest. Hope they work the bugs out.

The caller ID showed that it was from an esteemed associate at the Academy, and I got so excited that I picked up the phone and gushed propofol-infused affection.

So I was more than receptive when my friend urged me to run again. "You were such a supporter of the museum, and we want to keep that on track. And we need your good green guidance in making that building as energy efficient as possible. You should run!"

And run I did, and a beautiful thing happened. Even though I had the advantage of incumbency, a woman that I have known, loved, and respected since she was eighteen prevailed, and the truth is, I couldn't have been happier.

Laura Dern was to be our next governor, and together with the amazing Annette Bening, she would make great things happen at the Academy.

As the next four years flew by, I felt an even stronger urge to get involved with the Academy again, especially the museum, as I had been in favor of it since its inception. Quite specifically, I wanted to ensure that we achieved, if not LEED Platinum status for the building, at least Gold or Silver.

I did the math of the three three-year terms of the governors, and knew that I wouldn't be running against Laura, Annette, or any female incumbent. So I threw my hat in the ring again, only to find that I was running against my good friend Whoopi Goldberg, who I first met in San Diego in 1978.

I used to be good at math, but not at this age, apparently, as the three-times tables were now proving challenging for me.

And to cut myself a bit of slack, during the "enter your name here to opt in" process, they do not list the incumbent.

After you've opted in, and they narrow it down to the top vote getters, *then* you see who the incumbent is, and not before.

Then the national tragedy of George Floyd's murder rocked our nation and the world, and some changes began to occur that were long overdue.

Were there a mechanism in place to remove my name from the ballot, I would have implemented it.

But the truth is . . . it was not needed. Everyone voted for Whoopi, including me.

And as a result, *real* change *began* to occur at the Academy, as they *began* at the networks, and at the studios. And we now have a more inclusive system than we have ever seen.

It's a good start. Let's keep at it.

Sleeping with My Ex

I STARTED SLEEPING WITH MY ex-wife again, over a decade ago. Proving that my current wife, Rachelle, is extremely open-minded.

I promise I'll return to that, but first let me tell you a tale that verifies that I have very good taste in picking a spouse. Twice.

Kudos must also be given to my grown children for accepting (most of) my romances since their mother and I split in 1988.

But this chapter goes back even further than that, back to 1978, when we were all living in an apartment above Jeff Goldblum.

We lived there about a year, but my kids brought me increasingly good luck (as children often do), and we soon moved into our first home in Hancock Park.

We now had our own backyard, vegetable garden, composting bins, woodworking shop, and swing set, given to us by my dear friend, Howard Hesseman, who passed a few days before I wrote these very words.

I was newly sober, and the house, the shop, the garden, and the family were things I always wanted, and now they were mine.

Would it be enough?

I had tried to get sober starting in 1976, and managed to put together about twenty-one days, then went back out again after realizing that I could have "a little wine with dinner."

That would work for a week, or two . . . and then it was right back to a quart of vodka, some coke, some pot, until the inevitable a few months later, and another promise to Ingrid that I would change.

There are support groups available to those mired in this struggle, and I continued to seek their help, but after my fifth attempt at getting sober, this fellow Billy Boyle, sober for many years, could no longer remain silent as I came in yet again.

He stood about five foot six, quite thin, with an equally thin mustache, and he was rarely without a cigarette.

"Welcome back, Slim," he said once more. "What is this, your fifth or sixth attempt at sobriety?" Before I could even answer, he went on, "You know you're never going to get sober, right?"

I was shocked. That was not the sort of greeting I had received the other four times I came in, battered and bruised, both emotionally and physically. I was slightly indignant. "What a terrible thing to say, Billy. Why would you say that?"

"Because it's true," he said. "You still doing that series at Universal?"

"*Battlestar Galactica*? Yeah, why?" I asked.

"You still married to . . . Gretchen?" Billy asked.

"Ingrid. Yeah," I responded.

"Two kids now, and a place in Hancock Park?" said Billy.

"Uh-huh." I wondered where this was headed.

"Oh, you're screwed," he reasoned. "You'll never get sober."

"I'm not sure I see your point," I said.

"Because you haven't lost anything," he explained, and he went on. "Come see me after you lose the wife, the house, the kids . . . all of it. Because you will."

He then took a deep drag on his smoke and awaited my reaction, which was stunned silence. Seeing I hadn't a worthy rebuttal, he continued.

"Here's the way it's going to work going forward," he instructed, pointing his finger and lit cigarette at my chest. "Next time you feel the need to drink . . . you will call me! Before you take a drink, not after, or

I'll come over there and kick your ass. Do you understand what I just said to you?"

In case you'd forgotten, Billy is five foot six, 110 pounds. I'm six foot four, 210 pounds.

"Okay, Billy. You're going to kick my ass. So—"

He quickly interrupted me. "You will call me *before* you drink."

"I will call you before I drink," I promised.

A few months go by. I stay sober, and all seems well, and then it happens . . .

Not some tragedy like losing a part, or a loved one, or learning that your mother is not your mother.

A good thing. Which is sure to trigger an alcoholic as much as a catastrophe.

I find myself at LAX early one morning in November 1978. I was on my way to Cuernavaca, Mexico, to begin work on *The In-Laws*, with Peter Falk and Alan Arkin.

This is the first big film I've done since I worked on *Goin' South* with Jack Nicholson and, more importantly, Jack's uncle Shorty George Smith, who I attempted to unseat in the Smirnoff Summer Open in Durango, Mexico.

How do you not drink in Mexico? How do you not drink with the pressure of working with two screen legends, Peter Falk and Alan Arkin?

How do you not drink when they've hired a blond actor (me), but the actor arriving in a few hours (also me) is now a redhead?

I had worked on *Elvis* with Kurt Russell, playing his drummer, a gentleman with decidedly dark hair. So they dyed my hair black, promising it would be returned to normal when I was done shooting. Which was night shooting, as in last night, just a few hours before my flight.

My hair did not return to blond, as promised, but was now as red as a baboon's ass. The stress was too much for me. It was time to double down with some equally red Bloody Marys and just loosen up the nerves a bit.

I ordered the drink and brought it up to my lips, and then I remembered . . .

Billy goddamned Boyle.

This is 1978, so there were no cell phones, but there was a pay phone nearby, and I dialed him up. And woke him up: "Who's this?"

"Billy, it's Ed Begley. You said to call you before I drink, so I'm here at LAX, and I'm calling you."

I was expecting great urgency from him, but his response was anything but.

"Okay, where you headed?"

"Mexico City. Then on to Cuernavaca," I answered, but I was thrown. Did he think I was asking him about 18 down on the crossword?

"I hear it's pretty there, especially in November. Give me a ring when you get settled," he said while actually yawning.

"Maybe I'm not telling this right," I said "I'm at LAX, and they just opened the bar at Terminal 2. I've already ordered a drink . . . hold on."

The pay phone was close enough that I could easily communicate with the barkeep. "Excuse me, did I just order a Bloody Mary?"

The bartender picked up my drink to show me. "It's right here. You coming back?"

"Did you get that?" I asked, returning the phone to my ear.

"I got it. You ordered a Bloody Mary. And, like I said, call me when you get to Mexico City."

This little prick was starting to piss me off. I looked at my boarding pass and confirmed my seating.

"And I'm seated in first, so besides the drink now, I'm going to have all the free drinks they'll serve me on the plane, and all you want is for me to call you when I land."

"Yes. Because you're not going to drink in the bar, and you're not going to drink on the plane, you dumb fuck, and do you know why?"

Now I was truly thrown. But I eventually got out a timid "Why."

"Because you called me."

He let that sink in, then went on. "If you really wanted to drink, you would have already had one. And you wouldn't have called me. If you really wanted to drink, you wouldn't have walked into that first meeting two years ago. *You don't want to drink.*"

Those last words somehow surprised me, but I knew they were true.

"I'll talk to you in a few hours. I'm going back to sleep." And he hung up.

I walked over and paid the bartender, who oddly didn't seem thrown by this ridiculous exchange.

And I drank only water on the flight, as I did on the entire shoot in Mexico. And when I got back to L.A., I initiated a new regimen of attending a meeting every single day, with no exceptions.

At some point, I knew that I had to get a sponsor and work the steps, but my career was surging! I had very different work requirements than the others in the meetings. My life was unique and special. I would get to that when I could.

Billy Boyle started to hound me about sponsorship and step work, and I just couldn't seem to make him understand how different my life was from all those others in the rooms.

And surprise of surprises . . .

I secretly drank again in my woodworking shop in the garage.

But what is so great about that last experiment with "normal" drinking, or any drinking, is that I was actually able to do it . . . for only three miserable days.

It was December 18, 1979, and I had bought a case of wine to give as Christmas gifts. I stored it out in the garage and was actually distributing it as intended to different agents and studio personnel as a thank-you for our work together over the year.

But my stress level had soared after we bought the house five months previous, and the minute that escrow closed, my work slowed to a trickle, and I was starting to panic about losing my home.

And if you're an alcoholic, what better way to make yourself more desirable to potential employers than to start drinking again.

Undeterred, I opened a bottle of wine and had a glass, and a second, and tried to drink a third but could not finish it because it had somehow gone bad. Odd.

Night two, I decided to dig deeper into the mystery of how last night's bottle had turned sour.

I opened the case and found an identical bottle to the one I had opened the previous night. I carefully inspected the cork before removal. I took a sniff after opening. It smelled fine, so I poured a glass, let it breathe, then drank a glass, then another, then . . . same thing. Something was off. I didn't feel well.

Was someone trying to poison me? I further inspected the cork to see if I could detect a small hole where someone had used a syringe to inject something into the bottle.

What was truly confusing was that these small "normal" amounts of wine were proving too much for me. One afternoon in 1977, Nelson Lyon and I drank *way* more than three glasses of wine.

We each drank six.

Not six glasses. We each drank six *bottles* of wine.

But what was happening now? Hold on . . . I had heard of this. Some folks were born with *or developed* an allergy to tannins. That must have happened to me in the past year while I had been sober!

I knew there was a logical explanation!

No more wine for me. I'll switch to beer. No tannins.

Day three of my drinking experiment took me to Gower Gulch and an early dinner at the Japanese restaurant there. I ordered my vegetable sushi and a nice cold Kirin, which I knew to be a quality brew.

They served it in a chilled glass, and it looked delicious. I took a nice pull on it, and it tasted great!

Now we're talking. I will stay away from the grape and stick with the grains.

But after about ten minutes of avocado roll and beer, I realized that I had somehow also developed an allergy to hops and barley.

I paid the check and climbed in my car to head home, which was not far from the restaurant. But after just a couple of blocks, I had to pull over.

Had I somehow brought a bottle of Kirin in the car with me and spilled it? My car reeked of beer.

I rubbed my hands on my face and I could smell the beer. It seemed to be coming out of my pores. If Ingrid's keen nose got a whiff of me, I was dead.

I would try again tomorrow with another alcoholic beverage—hey, maybe vodka would do the trick—but first, I needed a shower.

As I walked in the front door, I could see that Ingrid was in the kitchen cooking, so I made a beeline for the bathroom. She spotted me but thankfully was occupied with setting a dish on the table.

But then she got her first really good look at me and moved in closer. "Are you okay? You don't look well."

But as she got a few feet away, a look of panic set in. "Oh my God, no! You're drinking again! Are you drinking again?"

"Drinking? Why do you say that? Why would I be drinking?"

"You are. You're drinking and now you're lying. I can't do this again," she wailed.

"Calm down," I said, genuinely moved by her reaction. "I am. I was. For just a couple of days. Just beer and wine . . . "

She cut me off. "Just beer and wine? Listen to yourself. You can never drink normally again!"

"You're right! I'm going to stop right now. Tonight. I'm going straight from here to a meeting. You can even drive me there." I tossed her my keys. "Just answer me one question . . . how did you know I was drinking?"

"You seriously don't know?" she asked.

Seeing that I hadn't a clue, she continued, "Your face changes. It started doing that a few years ago. I'm surprised you never noticed."

I seriously had no idea what she was talking about. "Changed how? What do you mean my face changes?"

"You look like one of the guys chasing after the wench, or trying to get the keys from the dog in the burning jailhouse . . . help me out here . . . the ride . . . at Disneyland!"

"Pirates of the Caribbean," I offered.

"Yes! Pirates of the Caribbean. You look like that."

I had just turned thirty a few months before this, so I was slightly offended but happy to change the topic from alcohol to audio-animatronics.

So I went to the closest mirror, and sure enough, there was Roy Disney, or one of his cousins perhaps, but definitely a man in his fifties staring back at me.

So I was handed yet another reason to get sober and stay sober.

An actor's vanity.

And I would look like that permanently soon enough.

Fortunately, my now-grown children, Amanda and Nick, were quite young at that time and missed that exchange, and a few others. But there were other things that they saw and heard that I wished they hadn't.

Though I made some bad decisions in my young life, I'd like to think I've learned and grown a bit since then.

And I find little purpose in dwelling on those bad decisions any more. I prefer instead to focus on my three very best decisions: Amanda, Nicholas, and Hayden.

Amanda has been a lifelong environmental activist. She received her master's degree in urban sustainability and currently works at one of my favorite green nonprofits in L.A., TreePeople. She has done more to make Los Angeles a better place than any six people I know, including me.

Nicholas studied physics at Reed College, then received his degree in electrical engineering at Portland State, and continues to work in that exciting field to this day. He also has three magnificent children of his own: Ellison, River, and Ari. I fancy myself an okay writer, and his sisters are great writers, but Nick puts all of us to shame.

Hayden is my youngest, and (thankfully) she got her mother's looks and passion for singing. She is truly a great singer and a great songwriter. And she has written a script so good, I predict it will come out before this book does. And if that were not enough, she has studied with my dear friend John Kirby for years and has become a terrific actress.

Let me close this chapter with the story of a road trip with Rachelle, my current wife; Ingrid, my ex-wife; and Hayden, my daughter, that really proves my good taste in women.

It was 2006, and my oldest daughter, Amanda, was soon to be wed.

A date was selected, as was a venue in Bend, Oregon.

Since I rarely fly, my wife Rachelle and I, and our six-year-old daughter Hayden, were going to drive up to Bend. When my ex-wife Ingrid learned of this, she said: "Ooh-ooh! Can I bum a ride?"

I said yes without thinking. My ex-wife in the back with my six-year-old, and my current wife up front with me, all ladies united against a common enemy.

Who could pass up an offer like that?

The general tone of the trip can be summed up by the following . . . an actual quote:

"Is he still doing that? Imagine what it was like when he had hair and a career?"

You can make Bend, Oregon, from Los Angeles in one day, but it's much easier to break it up and stop somewhere halfway, which is what we did.

As we checked in to the Best Western in Shasta, I asked my ex, Ingrid, what kind of bed she wanted for her room, and she said, "Don't bother. We can all just share a room."

Like I learned in improv class . . . always agree.

It got even better when we turned in for the night.

It was determined by the two grown ladies that Hayden would sleep with me, and they would share the other bed.

Which they did, and for inspiration they stayed up late watching *The War of the Roses*. I'm sure you know the general tone of that film: a divorce so nasty that reasonable people are driven to attempted murder.

But it is somehow a great comedy. As was that whole trip, and the wonderful healing time we had together, and thank God we had that, before Ingrid passed away a few months later.

Laughter can heal many wounds, and it certainly has helped me through troubling times.

I said at the beginning of this chapter that I started sleeping with my ex again over a decade ago, and though the Bend, Oregon, trip does meet those standards, I actually slept with my ex last night, too. And the night before.

I feel quite honored that my grown kids have entrusted me with a beautiful urn that sits in my man cave and is as good a focal point as any to remember the kind and gentle spirit that was their mother.

Peachtree Battle

I BLAME MAURICE LAMARCHE.

Maurice is a brilliant voice-over actor and one of Howie Mandel's closest friends since the seventies, and, like Howie, my dear friend since the early eighties.

And Maurice, in turn, introduced me to one Rachelle Diane Carson.

Thanks, Maurice!

See, in print, that exclamation mark could signify "Thank you for connecting me to the love of my life!"

Or it could mean "Thanks for nothing, Maurice!"

I'll let you decide after you've finished this chapter.

I've been to Atlanta many times over the years, and there must be fifty streets that are named "Peachtree" something.

The one that always tickled me was Peachtree Battle.

I suppose it was named after some skirmish that occurred during the Civil War, but whatever the origin, I found myself one lovely Georgia peach who is not afraid to battle.

Rachelle was actually raised in Buckhead, which is funny because her pet name for me rhymes with Buckhead.

Though I am sincere in my gratitude toward Maurice, I must concede that things didn't start well with Rachelle and me.

Sure, that first lunch with Maurice went fine. We dined at a nice little spot in West Hollywood, and Rachelle was quite fascinating. An actress for years, sober for years, quite funny, and quite attractive. Besides being a working actress, she had a second career teaching Pilates.

She was herself an ideal calling card for that side hustle. Women would often be heard to say, "Can you make me look like that?" while looking her up and down.

After lunch with Maurice, numbers were exchanged, and I wound up calling her after a reasonable period of time.

It was about eight thirty on a weeknight, and I had just gotten off work and was pleased that I had caught her at home, and that she had picked up the phone, hearing that it was me.

I asked if she wanted to grab a bite sometime, and she said yes, and then, driven by what I felt was a moment of spontaneity, I offered a friendly amendment.

"Hey, I just got off work, and I'm actually really hungry now . . . do you want to grab a bite tonight?"

Total silence for a bit, then, "Well, I think that's highly inappropriate." Those were her exact words: *highly inappropriate*. And it wasn't so much the words as it was the feeling behind those words . . . I had clearly pissed her off. Full Glenn Close. 0 to 60.

I apologized profusely and promised to call again with better notice, but that would have proved challenging, as that slip of paper had now been reduced to a fine powder by my young and nimble fingers.

To this day, I contend that it was just an innocent bit of spontaneity. She is steadfast in her belief that it was a booty call.

For the record, I always thought that a booty call took place a good deal later than eight thirty. And it most certainly did not involve dining at a fine restaurant, which was the offer on the table on that particular evening . . . along with the white linen.

We will never agree on that one, and probably many others, but it mattered not, as she moved to Canada and moved on to a serious relationship that lasted several years. I wound up in a serious relationship or two myself, as she and I were simply not meant to be.

But on November 7, 1993, I was the emcee of an event for Friends of the River at the Barker Hangar in Santa Monica, and who should be manning a table of auction items but one Rachelle Diane Carson.

I apologized for my part in the confusion two years earlier, we both finished our chores at the event, and I gave spontaneity one more shot, and this time it worked.

She agreed to join me at Matteo's in Westwood, which was on the way home for both of us. I had dinner and a business meeting planned with Bernard, the former maître d' at Spago, who was opening a restaurant across from Morton's at Melrose and Robertson.

We spent about an hour at Matteo's and then . . . I somehow convinced her to come back to my place in the Valley and "run lines."

How this worked on a woman who had previously exhibited fairly sensitive smoke-and-mirror detectors for my blarney, I do not know. But she knowingly allowed me to pluck the batteries out of those warning devices, one by one.

I hope I have not been crass in the prior chapters of this book, and I don't intend to start now, but Rachelle is very special, and we have always had something very special.

A deep attraction that I truly believe now was part of a series of events, timed in such a way that Hayden would be the end result.

And for reasons unclear to me, I fought my bashert, my destiny, for the next three years that we saw each other.

It is my memory that we split up twenty different times in those three years.

To illustrate what lengths I would go to, and what depths I would sink to, in fighting what was clearly my fate, I'll offer the following true story. And there's no way to spin it where I don't come off like a total weasel, so let's just get it over with.

Rachelle was to do the national tour in a production of *Dial M for*

Murder as the understudy for her friend Nancy Allen, who was playing the female lead opposite Roddy MacDowell.

We attended Peter Falk's birthday party the night before and had a lovely time, and then after a few hours' sleep, I drove her to LAX to catch an early flight to begin the tour.

The minute I got home from dropping her off for a months-long commitment from which she could not easily return . . . I called up AT&T and changed my number.

Cold, I know, but I had been trying to end it for a while, and I hadn't the willpower, so I wanted to eliminate that option for her, so we could finally put an end to this madness.

I never weakened and called her, and there was no way for her to call me, so we somehow got through a month or two without having any communication, and then . . . I got a postcard!

It was an announcement card telling me that she was "going on" for Nancy as the female lead in *Dial M for Murder.* But it was not one of those mass-mailing announcement cards. It was handwritten and had a personal message to me.

I realized the second that I saw it that I actually *did* want to hear from her, and I must have stopped myself from boarding a train and surprising her about a dozen times.

I remained strong.

Until I wasn't.

A few months later, I was traveling to Washington, D.C., by train, and she somehow knew this, and made it known that she would be in nearby Philadelphia.

We arranged to meet, and did, and finally had that moment of absolute clarity that we're sometimes graced with.

And I dove off the emotional high-dive, hoping that someone would fill the pool with water before I landed . . . and they did.

And the one with her hand on the fire hose was my dear Rachelle. And I suddenly felt safe.

I decided to stop fighting a good thing when it's sitting right there in front of me.

Now that I have the luxury of hindsight, let me make a short list of some of the other things that I was dead set against at the time.

"I will never move from this house."

"I will never marry again."

"I will never have more kids."

Well, I would absolutely have more kids, or kid. The amazing Hayden Begley, who along with her brother and sister brings more joy to my life than I can ever imagine.

I positively would and did marry again, at a chapel just down the street from where my first wife Ingrid and I were wed. And we would all become friends, and laugh together, and welcome grandchildren into the world together.

I absolutely would and did move from that house that I lived in for twenty-six years, the longest I've lived anywhere. But thanks to Rachelle, I would find even greater happiness in my LEED Platinum home on the most beautiful peaceful street in the San Fernando Valley.

My dreams have all been for pence, and my destiny has always been delivered in pounds.

And it somehow continues, to this day.

Jerry Lee Lewis

I HAVE NEVER MET JERRY Lee Lewis.

I don't really have any stories about Jerry Lee Lewis.

And this chapter doesn't really have anything to do with Jerry Lee Lewis.

Other than prompting this likely exchange:

Q. What does Ed Begley Jr. have in common with Jerry Lee Lewis?

A. There's a whole lot of shaking going on.

Though I would not be officially diagnosed until August 2016, when the world was a different place in so many ways, I knew that something was up in 2004.

I had lost about half of my sense of taste and half of my sense of smell. I was having trouble with my balance and had a small and intermittent tremor in my left thumb and forefinger.

A trip to Vancouver one morning in 2004 certainly got my attention. I was looking forward to the drive, but they needed me the following day, so I got on a plane. But about a minute after liftoff, the plane pitched violently to the port side and plummeted from the sky, no longer a plane but now more like a feathered brick.

All I could muster was a very loud "Oh, boy!"

Which caused everyone ahead of me to subtly turn and look in my direction, hoping there wasn't going to be any trouble. As it turns out, the plane wasn't falling, I was. Or more accurately, I *thought* I was. I was actually upright, strapped into my seat.

That event, and the other conditions, caused my doctor to eventually order an MRI to rule out a brain lesion or a tumor. Fortunately, the scan showed no tumors.

So I went about my business, riding my bike up to Mulholland and around the lake in Franklin Canyon, going to the gym every day, eating super healthy, as always. It all probably worked in my favor, keeping the more severe manifestations of the disease at bay for nearly twelve years.

But then in 2016, things got harder to ignore.

I was constantly having to go back to the chiropractor, as my shoulder had lost a great deal of the range of motion. I had somehow pulled a muscle yet again, on my left side.

I had to be fitted for a special boot, as I kept tearing a muscle in my left foot, or was it the Achilles tendon? And I finally saw a pattern emerge . . . all of these muscle "injuries" were happening on my left side. Odd coincidence, it seemed.

I finally had to go to a speech therapist, as I was starting to slur my words, and I needed some help with vocal exercises to keep that at bay. *Probably my age*, I thought. None of us are young forever.

After just one session, this speech therapist contacted my doctor, who suggested that I see a top neurologist at Cedars-Sinai.

I did. I then saw a second neurologist at UCLA, and both confirmed the diagnosis of Parkinson's, and things just got weirder every day for the remainder of 2016, for all the obvious reasons.

For my part, I was content to do what the neurologist recommended and nothing more. "I'll probably be dead in a year or three, like my dear friend Bob Hoskins. So what's the point?" I was heard to say.

But my wife of nearly twenty-two years can best be described by my friend Don Henley's song: "I will not go quietly."

She would not go quietly during the first three years we were dating but not yet married.

She would not go quietly with my "I'm not having any more kids" declaration during that same period. Nor would she surrender on finding us a new and better home.

She scoured the internet, talked to dozens of specialists knowledgeable in neurological matters, sharing news of alternative treatments that can complement the standard and effective treatment for Parkinson's, which is carbidopa/levodopa.

And that has proved to be a winning combination.

I've had it since 2004. I was officially diagnosed in 2016, and I still ride a bike every day, go to the gym, eat healthy, and I'm working as much as I have at any point in my life.

With this book, my condition will probably become widely known. And that's fine with me.

As of this writing, I am still able to learn lines, and I'm still ambulatory to such a degree that I can perform most tasks asked of a seventy-four-year-old.

Which included roller skating in a series I had recently called *Bless This Mess*! I've still got it!

Parkinson's, I mean.

But even with all that, it's still quite sublime.

I realized early on that I had won the lottery, being born Ed Begley's son.

That doors would open, and traffic violations, and even traffic accidents, were easily resolved.

For others, not so much.

How can we possibly fix that, and all the other problems in the world? Social justice, climate change, hunger, homelessness?

For me, the only way to ready myself for that kind of work is to recognize:

That this is it, as I finish this humble memoir.

Though I certainly remember the past, and plan for the future, I try not to spend too much time dwelling on either.

I urge you to do the same.

Focusing on your breath and nothing else is a good start.

Let everything else slip away.
You might just find yourself present for this moment:
Right.
Now.
Where we all visualize a better world.
And then we strive to make it so.

Acknowledgments

It had long been suggested that I write a memoir, but I could never seem to put pen to paper, or fingers to keyboard, and actually begin.

So I must credit my daughter Hayden for finally motivating me. She showed up one day, armed with her smartphone and a simple goal. I would sit there and tell the full and complete story of my seventy-three years in Hollywood. Or at least as much as her data plan and battery would allow.

But to be fair, it all really started a year prior to that.

For that is when the remarkable literary agent David Vigliano reached out to me and suggested I write a memoir. A suggestion that came with the generous offer of connecting me with a ghostwriter.

But now that I think of it, I didn't know David Vigliano at the time, so to give credit where it's due, I must thank and acknowledge Brett Dalton, Rachelle's dear friend and financial adviser.

But as I began taking notes to one day turn over to this ghostwriter, I soon became aware that it was *way* too much fun to turn over to *anyone*, and I was going to write it all myself. I soon had forty-five pages of notes that were not so much notes as they were actual chapters of a book.

I then asked a few dear friends (and wonderful writers) to give it a read, and their input proved invaluable.

Thank you, Dave Mirkin, Bruce Wagner, Wallace Shawn, Dennis

Acknowledgments

Klein, Bill Bentley, and Marc Vahanian for giving me your time and laughing at all the right places.

To Rebecca De Mornay, for making Harry Dean Stanton so happy for so many years.

To Brad Koepenick, for his vital help with this book, and for being such an amazing friend and mentor to Hayden over the years.

To Bradley Lane, Dave Pabian & Teri Karshner for inspiring me at Valley College, and beyond.

To Don Henley, for saving Walden Woods and allowing me to be part of it. And then there's the matter of being one of the greatest singer-songwriters ever. And a great and loyal friend.

And while we're on the subject of musical geniuses, thank you, Tom Waits. For introducing me to Ingrid, my first wife. And inspiring me as a musician and an actor.

To my dear friend Cheryl Tiegs, for throwing me the best birthday of my life, my fiftieth.

To Cindy and Alan Horn, for partnering with Cheryl to give me that same wonderful birthday, and for conspiring with Norman and Lyn Lear to do such important environmental work for the past four decades.

To my agents and managers from my younger years, Mike Belson and Eric Klass; Jason Winters and Erik Sterling; and Jon Carrasco and Stephen Roseberry. The fact that they are still a part of my life speaks volumes as to what a good job they did for me in my youth.

To Dick Stahl, for uttering the line that is the title of the book.

To Gita and Mukesh, for bringing the perfect balance of meditation, mangoes, and Mulligatawny to my life.

To Pam Grier, for still taking my calls, even though we're not on a show at this precise moment.

To Wendie Malick, for taking my calls while we *are* on a show together.

To Paula Poundstone, who I should probably devote an entire book to . . . not just this acknowledgment. I love you, Paula!

To Anthony Turk, for always making certain that they do *not* send a car to pick me up.

Acknowledgments

To Chuck Lorre and Steve Molaro, for giving me the best job I could imagine these past five years.

To Vince Gilligan and Peter Gould, for allowing me into the *Better Call Saul* family, where I got to do work that I didn't think possible in these, my twilight years.

To David O. Russell, for making nothing but great movies. And even allowing me to be in one of them: *Amsterdam*.

To Chelsea Handler, for providing such inspiration with her great books, and for providing a shower when I'd arrive by bike.

To Dave Lederman, for getting me all those wonderful jobs, and many more.

To Keith Addis and Mike Abrams, for keeping me gainfully employed these past twelve years. And for getting this book back on track when I was headed in the wrong direction.

To Jarlath Dorney, who exemplifies all that is great about the Irish.

To the Hachette Book Group, and specifically Brant Rumble, for being so incredibly helpful and encouraging at every step of the way.

To Eric and Tania, Peter and Wendie, Bruce and Jamie, Gavin and Yukimi, Dave and Savanah, and of course Bev, for bringing so much laughter and music into my life.

To the center of my life and inspiration at every turn, my three perfect children, Nicholas, Amanda, and Hayden.

To my amazing grandchildren, Ellison, River, and Ari.

And of course, to my hysterically funny and amazingly beautiful wife Rachelle. You bring me more joy than you probably know.